*Firm in the faith*

# Firm in the faith

## A training manual for Christian growth

### Student's book

### Dennis D. Hustedt

 EVANGELICAL PRESS

EVANGELICAL PRESS
Faverdale North Industrial Estate, Darlington, DL3 0PH, England

Evangelical Press USA
P. O. Box 84, Auburn, MA 01501, USA

e-mail: sales@evangelical-press.org
web: http://www.evangelicalpress.org

First published 2000

**British Library Cataloguing in Publication Data available**

ISBN 0 85234 457 0

Printed and bound in Great Britain by Creative Print & Design Wales, Ebbw Vale.

# Contents

# Introduction

This book is an introduction to Christian theology. These lessons will help you learn the basic doctrines (beliefs) of the Christian faith.

Each week we shall answer one catechism question. A catechism is a series of questions and answers which explain established doctrinal truths from the Bible. Catechism questions and answers help us to understand what the Bible teaches, and what we should believe as Christians.

The catechism questions in this book are based on the *Westminster Shorter Catechism*. In England, in 1647, a group of Christian ministers met to discuss their concern about the lack of sound teaching of the Word of God. In response, they wrote both a confession of faith and a larger and shorter catechism. For hundreds of years young people in churches in English-speaking countries all over the world have memorized the catechism as part of their training in the Christian faith. The shorter catechism contains 107 catechism questions and answers. I have selected forty-eight of those catechism questions for this book. I strongly encourage you to memorize them along with the forty-eight accompanying Bible verses. The seven questions included in each lesson will help you to understand the catechism question and answer. Answer them to the best of your ability. At the end of each lesson you will find a variety of activities: different stories of great Christians of the past, hymns and choruses, crosswords and word searches, and discussion topics. These activities will help you to apply the truths taught in the catechism, and to use your Bible when solving problems.

This material is able to transform your life, so do your best to learn it thoroughly and to make it a part of you. You can never pursue anything greater than knowing the God of the Bible. Many adults have used this material to increase their understanding of the Christian faith. We all, young and old, are on an important journey. May the Lord bless you on your personal pilgrimage!

# First Quarter

## The chief end of man

Memorize the following catechism answer and Bible memory verse:

### Catechism Question

'What is the chief end of man?'

### Answer

'The chief end of man is to glorify God and to enjoy him for ever.'

### Check it out for yourself

1. Read John 4:24; Acts 17:11; 1 Corinthians 10:31; Galatians 5:22-23 and 1Thessalonians 5:16-18. How can we glorify God?

2. Read 1 Peter 1:8-9 and 1 Thessalonians 5:16-18. How do we enjoy God?

3. Read John 17:24. Do you think God enjoys being glorified?

4. When you enjoy something how do you show it?

5. Read Colossians 3:16. Is it more enjoyable to glorify God on your own or with other Christians?

6. Read Luke 10:21. Do you think God is happy? Why?

7. Read Psalm 100. Does God want us to be happy? How do you know?

### Memory Verse

'So whether you eat or drink or whatever you do, do it all for the glory of God' (1 Cor. 10:31).

### Action

**Jesus shall reign**

**Isaac Watts (1674-1748)**

Isaac Watts was an outstanding Christian hymn-writer who lived in England. He wrote over 600 hymns including 'Joy to the world' and 'O God our help in ages

past'. A great hymn written by Watts is 'Jesus shall reign', based on Psalm 72 (written by Solomon). Read Psalm 72 and see if you can identify the verses on which this hymn is based. What was the hymn-writer wanting to convey?

Jesus shall reign where'er the sun
Does its successive journeys run;
His kingdom stretch from shore to shore
Till moons shall wax and wane no more.

For Him shall endless prayer be made,
And praises throng to crown his head;
His name, like sweet perfume, shall rise
With every morning sacrifice.

People and realms of every tongue
Dwell on his love with sweetest song;
And infant voices shall proclaim
Their early blessings on his name.

Blessings abound where'er he reigns;
The prisoner leaps to lose his chains;
The weary find eternal rest;
And all the sons of want are blessed.

## The Word of God

Memorize the following catechism answer and Bible memory verse:

### Catechism Question

'What book has God given to direct us how we may glorify and enjoy him?'

### Answer

'The Word of God, which is contained in the Old and New Testaments, is the only authority by which we are directed how we may glorify and enjoy him.'

**Check it out for yourself**

1. How many books of the Bible are there in the Old Testament? And in the New Testament?

2. Read Matthew 5:18; Luke 18:31; Luke 24:44-45. Are all the books of the Bible inspired? Why do you say so?

3. According to 2 Timothy 3:17, what is accomplished when the Word of God is at work in our lives?

4. Read 2 Peter 1:20-21. What do these verses teach us about the Holy Spirit's role in the writing of the Scriptures?

5. Read John 16:12-15 and Ephesians 6:17. What role does the Holy Spirit play when we read the Scriptures?

6. Which is your favourite book of the Bible? Why?

7. According to this catechism question, what is the result of knowing the Bible and allowing its truth to direct our lives?

### Memory Verse

'All Scripture is God-breathed and is useful for teaching, rebuking, correcting and training in righteousness' (2 Tim. 3:16).

1
2
3
4
5
6
7

Action

**Did you know. . .?**

- The printing press was invented in Germany in 1454, and the first book to be printed was the Gutenberg Bible.

- The Gutenberg Bible was printed in Latin, not German.

- Martin Luther, the great Reformer, translated the New Testament into German in just eleven weeks.

- The word 'Bible' comes from the Greek word for 'papyrus plant' (*biblos*), as the leaves of that plant were used for paper.

The primary teaching of Scripture

Memorize the following catechism answer and Bible memory verse:

**Catechism Question**

'What do the Scriptures primarily teach?'

**Answer**

'The Scriptures primarily teach what we are to believe about God, and what duty God requires of us.'

**Check it out for yourself**

1. Write down three important things the Bible teaches us about God. Discuss them.

2. The memory verse tells us that we should fear God. What does this mean?

3. Read Deuteronomy 6:24-25 and John 14:15. Why has God given us commandments to keep?

4. Read Deuteronomy 5:1-22. Who received the Ten Commandments from God? When and where did this take place?

5. Read Luke 10:25-27. List some of the duties which God requires of us.

6. Read Romans 8:12-14. Are we able to perform these duties in our own strength? Explain.

7. Read Deuteronomy 6:4-8. From these verses, can you explain why it is important to learn these catechism answers and memory verses?

**Memory Verse**

'Fear God and keep his commandments, for this is the whole duty of man' (Eccles. 12:13).

**Action**   Word Search
Ten Commandments

On the opposite page you will find ten hidden words. Each word is a key word found in one of the Ten Commandments (Exod. 20). When you find a word write it next to the correct commandment.

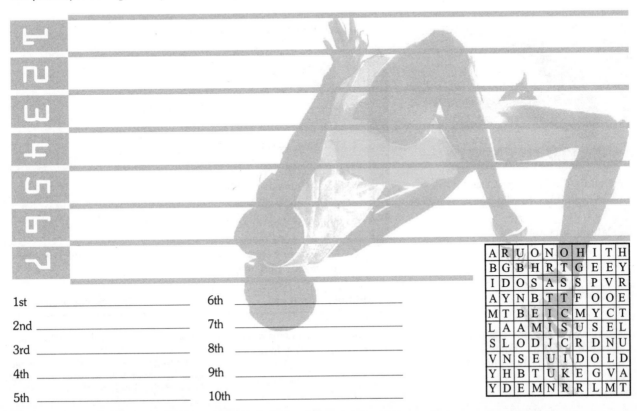

1st _____

2nd _____

3rd _____

4th _____

5th _____

6th _____

7th _____

8th _____

9th _____

10th _____

| A | R | U | O | N | O | H | I | T | H |
|---|---|---|---|---|---|---|---|---|---|
| B | G | B | H | R | T | G | E | E | Y |
| I | D | O | S | A | S | S | P | V | R |
| A | Y | N | B | T | T | F | O | O | E |
| M | T | B | E | I | C | M | Y | C | T |
| L | A | A | M | I | S | U | S | E | L |
| S | L | O | D | J | C | R | D | N | U |
| V | N | S | E | U | I | D | O | L | D |
| Y | H | B | T | U | K | E | G | V | A |
| Y | D | E | M | N | R | R | L | M | T |

## Who is God?

Memorize the following catechism answer and Bible memory verse:

### Catechism Question

'Who is God?'

### Answer

'God is a Spirit, infinite, eternal and unchangeable, in his being, wisdom, power, holiness, justice, goodness and truth.'

**Check it out for yourself**

1. What does Psalm 90:2 teach us about God?

2. And James 1:17?

3. How is God described in Exodus 3:14?

4. In Psalm 147:4-6?

5. And in Revelation 4:8?

6. Which of God's characteristics are listed in Exodus 34:6-7?

7. The memory verse is John 4:24. What do you think it means to worship God in spirit and truth?

### Memory Verse

'God is Spirit, and his worshippers must worship in spirit and in truth' (John 4:24).

### Action    The obvious response

Look at Revelation 4:8 again (Question 5) and then read verses 9-11. You will notice that the response of the living creatures in heaven is to worship and praise God. Refer back to Exodus 34:6-7

(Question 6) and then read verses 8-9. How did Moses respond to the greatness of God? He bowed to the ground at once and worshipped. To know God and to see him for who he really is will cause us to worship, praise and adore him. 'Now to the King eternal, immortal, invisible, the only God, be honour and glory for ever and ever. Amen' (1 Tim. 1:17).

Why do you think the hymn-writer, Walter Smith, wrote the hymn 'Immortal, invisible'?

**Immortal, invisible**

Immortal, invisible, God only wise,
In light inaccessible hid from our eyes,
Most blessed, most glorious, the Ancient of Days,
Almighty, victorious, Thy great name we praise.

## There is one God

Memorize the following catechism answer and Bible memory verse:

### Catechism Question

'Are there more gods than one?'

### Answer

'There is but one only, the living and true God.'

**Check it out for yourself**

1. In Acts 19:23-41 which goddess did the Ephesians worship? Why should we not worship this goddess today?

2. In 1 Kings 18:16-40 which god was being worshipped in Israel? What happened in this contest?

3. In Matthew 4:8-11 who wanted to be worshipped? How did Jesus respond?

4. In Philippians 3:18-19 which god is being worshipped?

5. In Matthew 6:24 which false god wants to master us? Explain how this can happen.

6. Are there gods that may tempt you to worship them rather than the true and living God? Explain.

7. What warning is given in Deuteronomy 8:19?

### Memory Verse

'Hear, O Israel, the LORD our God, the LORD is one' (Deut. 6:4).

### Action

There are hundreds of blessings promised to believers in Jesus when they love and follow the one, true God. Matthew 6:33 tells us not to worry as God has promised to supply all our needs if we seek his kingdom and righteousness

before all other things. He promises to give us joy and to bless us when we set our affection on him more than on anything else.

Do you know the chorus taken from Moses' song found in Deuteronomy 32:3-4?

**Chorus**

Ascribe greatness to our God, the Rock,
His work is perfect
    and all his ways are just. (repeat)
A God of faithfulness and without injustice;
Good and upright is he! (repeat)

**Deuteronomy 32:3-4**

Oh, praise the greatness of our God!
He is the Rock, his works are perfect,
    and all his ways are just.
A faithful God who does no wrong,
    upright and just is he!

## The Trinity

Memorize the following catechism answer and Bible memory verse:

### Catechism Question

'How many persons are there in the Godhead?'

### Answer

'There are three persons in the Godhead; the Father, the Son, and the Holy Spirit; and these three are one God, the same in substance, equal in power and glory.'

**Check it out for yourself**

1. The Bible teaches us that God exists as three persons (the Trinity), but that there is only one God. Explain what you think this means.

2. Can you name any religious cults who consider themselves to be Christian, but who deny the Trinity?

3. Read Luke 1:39-45. How many persons of the Trinity can you find in these verses?

4. Read Luke 1:67-69. How many persons of the Trinity can you find in these verses?

5. Read Matthew 3:16-17. Which persons of the Trinity were present at the baptism of Jesus?

6. Read John 10:30-33. Did Jesus claim to be God? How do you understand verse 30?

7. Read John 14:15-20. What do these verses teach about the Trinity? Where should we desire to see the Holy Spirit dwelling?

### Memory Verse

'Therefore go and make disciples of all nations, baptizing them in the name of the Father and of the Son and of the Holy Spirit' (Matt. 28:19).

### Action
**The Trinity**

A diagram can never adequately represent how God exists in three persons: Father, Son and Holy Spirit. Two of the diagrams (opposite page) are incorrect, and the third one presents the Trinity in a way which conforms more accurately to the Bible's teaching on this subject.

Cross out the two incorrect diagrams and explain why they are wrong. Although our minds can never fully understand how one God can exist as three persons, we should not avoid discussion on this subject. It is a fundamental truth about God, and one which helps us to know him better. Make sure that you use your Bible to guide you in all your thinking.

| Diagram 1 | Diagram 2 | Diagram 3 |
|---|---|---|
| Father    Son   Holy Spirit | Father   Son   Holy Spirit | Father  GOD  Holy Spirit  Son |

## The decrees of God

Memorize the following catechism answer and Bible memory verse:

### Catechism Question

'What are the decrees of God?'

### Answer

'The decrees of God are his eternal purpose, by which, for his own glory, he has ordained whatever comes to pass.'

**Check it out for yourself**

1. What does the word 'sovereign' mean in Daniel 4:17, 25, 32? And 'decree' in Daniel 4:24, 31?

2. Read Daniel 1:1-2. Who was Nebuchadnezzar?

3. Read Daniel 4:4-18. Explain the dream in your own words.

4. Read Daniel 4:19-27. How did Daniel interpret the dream?

5. Read Daniel 4:28-33. What was Nebuchadnezzar's spiritual problem? What was his punishment?

6. Read Daniel 4:34-35. What did Nebuchadnezzar learn at the end of his punishment?

7. Read Daniel 4:36-37. After his sanity was restored, what kind of man was Nebuchadnezzar?

### Memory Verse

'He does as he pleases
    with the powers of heaven
        and the peoples of the earth.
No one can hold back his hand
    or say to him: "What have you done?"'
(Dan. 4:35).

### Action

**Did you know...?**

Nebuchadnezzar became King of Babylon after his father's death in 605 B.C. On 16 March 597 B.C., he captured Jerusalem and took Jehoiachin, King of Judah, and many of the Jewish people captive to Babylonia (2 Kings 24:8-17).

1 2 3 4 5 6 7

* Babylon, at the time of Daniel and the captivity of the Jews, was the largest city of the known world, covering more than 1000 hectares (2,500 acres).
* Babylon's name means 'gate of God'. The city's location is marked by a broad area of ruins just east of the Euphrates River, 90 km (56 miles) south of Baghdad, Iraq. Saddam Hussein and the Iraqi government have attempted to restore some of the magnificence of the ancient city.
* Legend credits Nebuchadnezzar with building one of the Seven Wonders of the World, the 'Hanging Gardens of Babylon'. He was an ambitious builder; he made Babylon one of the most magnificent cities of the ancient world.

## Creation

Memorize the following catechism answer and Bible memory verse:

### Catechism Question

'What is the work of creation?'

### Answer

'The work of creation is God, by his mighty power, making all things from nothing, in the space of six days, and all very good.'

**Check it out for yourself**

Read Genesis 1:1 - 2:3, the creation account, and summarize what occurred on each day of creation.

1. Genesis 1:1-5. Day 1

2. Genesis 1:6-8. Day 2

3. Genesis 1:9-13. Day 3

4. Genesis 1:14-19. Day 4

5. Genesis 1:20-23. Day 5

6. Genesis 1:24-31. Day 6

7. Genesis 2:1-3. Day 7

### Memory Verse

'By faith we understand that the universe was formed at God's command, so that what is seen was not made out of what was visible' (Heb. 11:3).

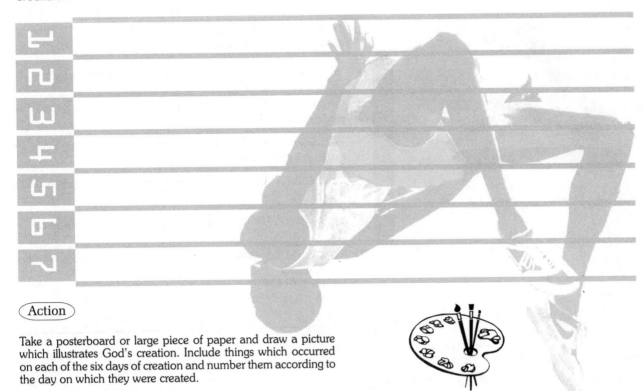

Action

Take a posterboard or large piece of paper and draw a picture which illustrates God's creation. Include things which occurred on each of the six days of creation and number them according to the day on which they were created.

## The image of God

Memorize the following catechism answer and Bible memory verse:

### Catechism Question

'How did God create man?'

### Answer

'God created man male and female, after his own image, in knowledge, righteousness, and holiness, with dominion over the creatures.'

### Check it out for yourself

1. Read Genesis 1:26. The verse begins: 'Then God said, "Let us..."'. To whom is God speaking?

2. What do you think it means to be made in God's image?

3. Read Ephesians 4:24. From this verse, what does it mean to be made in God's image?

4. Read Colossians 3:10. From this verse, what does it mean to be made in God's image?

5. Read 1 John 3:1-3. What does it mean to be made in God's image from these verses?

6. Read Psalm 8:3-8. What has God done for men and women?

7. Read Psalm 8:5. What does it mean to be 'crowned with glory and honour'?

### Memory Verse

'So God created man
in his own image,
in the image of God
he created him;
male and female
he created them' (Gen. 1:27).

### Action

**Bijago**

The story of the Bijago people is found in the book *You Too Can Change The World*.

The Bijagos Islands off the coast of West Africa have beautiful white, sandy beaches, palm trees, and brightly coloured birds. They belong to Guinea-Bissau, and the people who inhabit them are called Bijago. Although the

islands are lovely, the people who live there are very poor. Many live in round houses made of mud, with thatched roofs. The houses are dark inside and the villages are sometimes very dirty. The people are often ill; their crops are poor and their cattle very weak.

The Bijago are animists. They believe in a Great Spirit who made them but will not help them. Instead they think that this Great Spirit sends them punishment and disaster. They build elaborate temples of mud and thatch. In the middle of each temple is an altar surrounded by fetishes (things which are worshipped) and carved idols. The Bijago are afraid of the *iran* (evil spirits) and hope that by sacrificing animals and performing special ceremonies they will be kept from harm.

But forty years ago Christian visitors came to the island. They preached about Jesus, and some of the people learned to trust in the Saviour. These Christians also translated the Bible into the Bijago language. In 1973 Tear Fund helped them to dig a well in their village. What a difference clean, fresh water made to them! The village chief became a Christian and burned all his idols. The Bijago Christians were so happy that they danced and sang for joy. Now there are Christians on several of the islands. The image of God is being restored in the people known as Bijago!

## The Fall

Memorize the following catechism answer and Bible memory verse:

### Catechism Question

'Did Adam and Eve remain in the condition in which they were created?'

### Answer

'Adam and Eve, being left to the freedom of their own will, fell from the condition in which they were created by sinning against God.'

**Check it out for yourself**

1. Read Genesis 3:1-5. Did the serpent (the devil) tell Eve the truth? Did Eve die? Explain.

2. Read Genesis 3:6-7. Which sin did Adam and Eve commit? What caused them to sin?

3. Read Genesis 3:8-10. Do people hide from God as Adam and Eve did? Explain.

4. Read Genesis 3:11-13. Discuss Adam and Eve's responses to God's questions.

5. Read Genesis 3:14-19. In these verses, what did God curse and whom did he judge?

6. Read Genesis 3:20-24. What change took place because of the sin of Adam and Eve?

7. Read James 1:13-15 and Romans 6:23. What causes sin and what is the awful consequence of it?

### Memory Verse

'For as in Adam all die, so in Christ all will be made alive' (1 Cor. 15:22).

### Action

**Word puzzle**

Unscramble each of the words to form a verse which is found in the book of Romans. Then, in your own words, explain what you think the verse means.

**1**
**2**
**3**
**4**
**5**
**6**
**7**

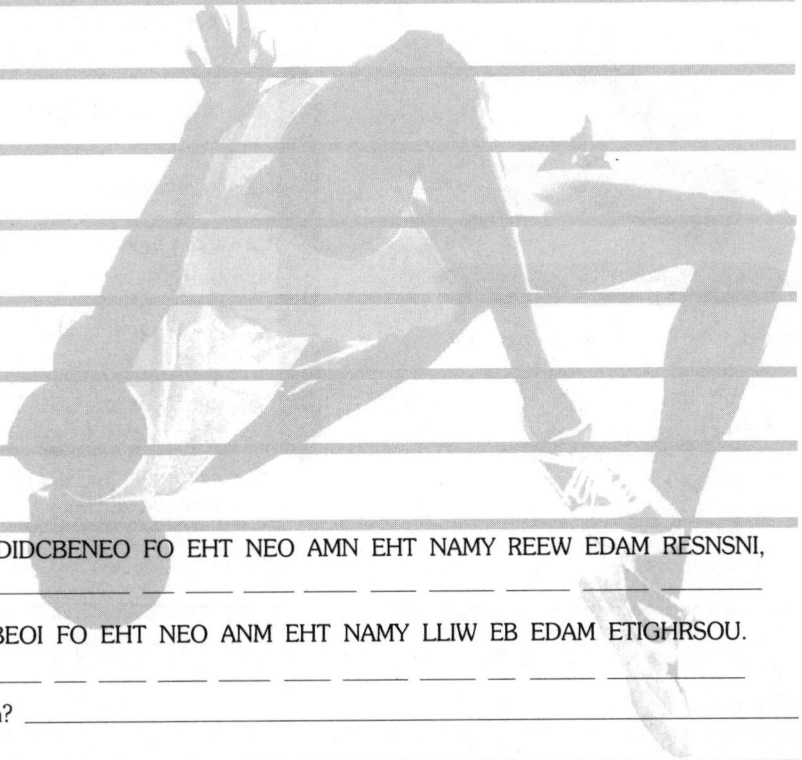

ORF SUJT SA OGHHTRU EHT SIEDIDCBENEO FO EHT NEO AMN EHT NAMY REEW EDAM RESNSNI,

___ ____ ___ _____ ___ _____ ____ _____ ___ ___ ___ ____ ____ ____ _____ ____

OS OALS RUGHHOT EHT NEDECBEOI FO EHT NEO ANM EHT NAMY LLIW EB EDAM ETIGHRSOU.

___ ____ _____ ___ _____ __ ___ ___ ___ ___ ____ __ ____ _____.

What does this unscrambled verse mean? _____

_____

## Sin

Memorize the following catechism answer and Bible memory verse:

### Catechism Question

'What is sin?'

### Answer

'Sin is not conforming to, or any breaking of, the law of God.'

**Check it out for yourself**

1. Read James 2:9-11. How many sins does a person need to commit to become a lawbreaker? Explain.

2. What do the Scriptures primarily teach?

3. Read Romans 3:20 and 7:7. What does the law do for us?

4. Read Romans 7:18-20. What is the problem with every human being?

5. Read Romans 6:5-7. How can we be free from the power of sin?

6. Read Romans 6:11-14. What practical steps can Christians take to avoid sinning against God?

7. Read Romans 8:12-14. What is the good news for Christians in these verses?

### Memory Verse

'Everyone who sins breaks the law; in fact, sin is lawlessness' (1 John 3:4).

### Action — Augustine (A.D. 354-430)

Augustine was the greatest of all the church fathers. As a young man, however, he was very sinful. He wrote about his sinful youth in a famous book called *The Confessions of Saint Augustine* in which he described how the Lord rescued him from sin and brought him into a life of grace and truth.

Augustine and his friends used to steal pears from a farmer's vineyard. Augustine wrote, 'I stole that which I had at home both in greater plenty and much better. I didn't care for that which I stole, I just took pleasure in the very theft and sin itself.' Although his father was a pagan, his mother was a godly woman who prayed earnestly for her son.

After moving from North Africa to Italy, he heard sermons from another famous theologian of the early church named Ambrose. Augustine realized that his problem was his sinful nature, 'a deformed soul'. He was convinced that he should begin studying the Scriptures. He came to realize not only how great his sin was, but also how much greater

God's grace was. At the age of thirty-one, Augustine was converted to Christ after much weeping and calling on God for deliverance. He went on to write many books about faith, which have been appreciated by Christians through the centuries.

## Christ the Redeemer

Memorize the following catechism answer and Bible memory verse:

### Catechism Question

'Who is the Redeemer of God's chosen people?'

### Answer

'The only Redeemer of God's chosen people is the Lord Jesus Christ, who, being the eternal Son of God, became man, and remains both God and man in one person for ever.'

### Check it out for yourself

1. Read 1 Timothy 2:5. What is a mediator?

2. Read John 1:1-5 and verse 14. Who is the Word and what is he like?

3. Read Luke 19:10 and John 3:16-17. What was Christ's purpose in coming into the world?

4. Read Luke 13:34-35. What did Jesus desire to do for Jerusalem? Was the city interested?

5. Read Luke 1:30-35. What is miraculous about the birth of Jesus?

6. Read Colossians 2:9. What does this verse teach us about Jesus?

7. Read Luke 1:67-69. What made Zechariah happy?

### Memory Verse

'But when the time had fully come, God sent his Son, born of a woman, born under law, to redeem those under law, that we might receive the full rights of sons' (Gal. 4:4-5).

### Action                    Crossword

This crossword contains the names of people who were directly involved in the Christmas story. Unscramble the letters in the shaded boxes to form a word which is central to our study. Write it on the line below.

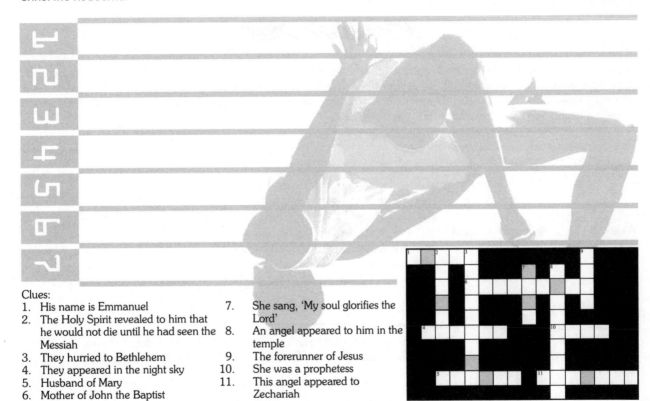

Clues:
1. His name is Emmanuel
2. The Holy Spirit revealed to him that he would not die until he had seen the Messiah
3. They hurried to Bethlehem
4. They appeared in the night sky
5. Husband of Mary
6. Mother of John the Baptist
7. She sang, 'My soul glorifies the Lord'
8. An angel appeared to him in the temple
9. The forerunner of Jesus
10. She was a prophetess
11. This angel appeared to Zechariah

## Time to review

This is a big week for you! Your work is to be reviewed. There are no questions to answer, just hard and intensive memory work to be done. The catechism answers and the Bible memory verses should become part of you, so don't lose the opportunity to hide God's Word in your heart. It will never fail to do you good, and it will bring glory to God. It would be wonderful if you had the opportunity to demonstrate your powers of memory to your friends, or to a wider audience. Seize the opportunity if it presents itself!

**Week 1:**   Q: 'What is the chief end of man?'
A: 'The chief end of man is to glorify God and to enjoy him for ever.'
Verse: 'So whether you eat or drink or whatever you do, do it all for the glory of God' (1 Cor. 10:31).

**Week 2:**   Q: 'What book has God given to direct us how we may glorify and enjoy him?'
A: 'The Word of God, which is contained in the Old and New Testaments, is the only authority by which we are directed how we may glorify and enjoy him.'
Verse: 'All Scripture is God-breathed and is useful for teaching, rebuking, correcting and training in righteousness' (2 Tim. 3:16).

**Week 3:**   Q: 'What do the Scriptures primarily teach?'
A: 'The Scriptures primarily teach what we are to believe about God, and what duty God requires of us.'
Verse: 'Fear God and keep his commandments, for this is the whole duty of man' (Eccles. 12:13).

**Week 4:**   Q: 'Who is God?'

A: 'God is a Spirit, infinite, eternal and unchangeable, in his being, wisdom, power, holiness, justice, goodness and truth.'

Verse: 'God is Spirit, and his worshippers must worship in spirit and in truth' (John 4:24).

**Week 5:**   Q: 'Are there more gods than one?'

A: 'There is but one only, the living and true God.'

Verse: 'Hear, O Israel, the LORD our God, the LORD is one' (Deut. 6:4).

**Week 6:**   Q: 'How many persons are there in the Godhead?'

A: 'There are three persons in the Godhead; the Father, the Son and the Holy Spirit; and these three are one God, the same in substance, equal in power and glory.'

Verse: 'Therefore go and make disciples of all nations, baptizing them in the name of the Father and of the Son and of the Holy Spirit' (Matt. 28:19).

**Week 7:**   Q: 'What are the decrees of God?'

A: 'The decrees of God are his eternal purpose, by which, for his own glory, he has ordained whatever comes to pass.'

Verse:

'He does as he pleases
    with the powers of heaven
    and the peoples of the earth.

No one can hold back his hand
    or say to him: "What have you done?"'

(Dan. 4:35).

**Week 8:**    Q: 'What is the work of creation?'

A: 'The work of creation is God, by his mighty power, making all things from nothing, in the space of six days, and all very good.'

Verse: 'By faith we understand that the universe was formed at God's command, so that what is seen was not made out of what was visible' (Heb. 11:3).

**Week 9:**    Q: 'How did God create man?'

A: 'God created man male and female, after his own image, in knowledge, righteousness, and holiness, with dominion over the creatures.'

Verse:

    'So God created man
      in his own image,
    in the image of God
      he created him;
    male and female
      he created them'

(Gen. 1:27).

Time to review

**Week 10:**   Q: 'Did Adam and Eve remain in the condition in which they were created?'
A: 'Adam and Eve, being left to the freedom of their own will, fell from the condition in which they were created by sinning against God.'
Verse: 'For as in Adam all die, so in Christ all will be made alive' (1 Cor. 15:22).

**Week 11:**   Q: 'What is sin?'
A: 'Sin is not conforming to, or any breaking of, the law of God.'
Verse: 'Everyone who sins breaks the law; in fact, sin is lawlessness' (1 John 3:4).

**Week 12:**   Q: 'Who is the Redeemer of God's chosen people?'
A: 'The only Redeemer of God's chosen people is the Lord Jesus Christ, who, being the eternal Son of God, became man, and remains both God and man in one person for ever.'
Verse: 'But when the time had fully come, God sent his Son, born of a woman, born under law, to redeem those under law, that we might receive the full rights of sons' (Gal. 4:4-5).

# Second Quarter

This is the start of a new quarter. During the next twelve weeks you will cover some of the doctrines concerning the person and work of the Lord Jesus Christ. These great truths are central to the faith. It is therefore essential to know and embrace them. Do not allow difficult theological concepts or terminology to discourage you. Knowledge of these doctrines will help you to mature in the faith, even if you have not had any theological training. Talk to your pastor or any other trained church leader if you have questions. All believers are learning together and growing in understanding of their faith.

## Christ's offices

Memorize the following catechism answer and Bible memory verse:

### Catechism Question

'What offices does Christ fulfil as our Redeemer?'

### Answer

'Christ, as our Redeemer, fulfils the offices of a prophet, a priest and a king, both while he was on earth and now in heaven.'

**Check it out for yourself**

1. Read Deuteronomy 18:14-22. What is the role of a prophet? How does Jesus fulfil that role?

2. Read Acts 3:22-26. How do Peter and Moses describe Jesus? In this role, what does Jesus do?

3. Read Hebrews 7:23-28. What is the role of a priest? How does Jesus fulfil this role?

4. Read Hebrews 4:14 - 5:10. How does the writer describe Jesus here? In this role, what does Jesus do ?

5. Read Psalm 2. What is the role of a king? How does Jesus fulfil this role?

6. Read Isaiah 9:1-7. How does Isaiah present the Lord Jesus? In this role, what does Jesus do ?

7. Read Matthew 12:15-21. Which of the three offices of Christ can you find in these verses?

### Memory Verse

'For to us a child is born,
  to us a son is given,
    and the government will be on his shoulders.
And he will be called
    Wonderful Counsellor, Mighty God,
    Everlasting Father, Prince of Peace'

(Isa. 9:6).

1
2
3
4
5
6
7

**Action**    **Prophets, priests and kings**

Here are some characters from the Old and New Testaments. Next to each name state whether the person was a prophet, a priest, or a king.

Eli _____    Josiah _____    Aaron _____

David _____    Miriam _____    Zephaniah _____

Anna _____    Ezra _____    Rehoboam _____

## Christ the Prophet

Memorize the following catechism answer and Bible memory verse:

### Catechism Question

'How does Christ fulfil the office of a prophet?'

### Answer

'Christ fulfils the office of a prophet because he has revealed to us, by his Word and Spirit, the will of God for our salvation.'

**Check it out for yourself**

1. Read Matthew 5:1-12. What is surprising about the people whom Jesus describes as blessed?

2. Read Matthew 5:21-32. How does Jesus' teaching differ from that of the Pharisees?

3. Read Matthew 5:33-48. How does Jesus' teaching differ from that of the Pharisees?

4. Read Matthew 6:1-15. How does Jesus' teaching differ from that of the Pharisees?

5. Read Matthew 6:19-34. What is Jesus teaching us about life in this world?

6. Read Matthew 7:15-23. Christ is a true prophet. How can we tell the difference between true and false prophets?

7. Read Matthew 7:24-29. What should we do in response to Christ's prophetic words? Why were Christ's listeners amazed in verse 29?

### Memory Verse

'No one has ever seen God, but God the one and only, who is at the Father's side, has made him known' (John 1:18).

### Action — True and false prophets

The Bible tells us that some prophets always spoke the true words of God, while others did not speak for God. Even today some people speak God's truth faithfully, but others speak falsely. The Scriptures warn us to watch out for false prophets. Indicate whether each person named below was a true prophet of God or a false prophet.

Isaiah _____        Jeremiah _____        Balaam _____

Hosea _____         Hymenaeus _____      Moses _____

Korah _____         Habakkuk _____       Elijah _____

## Christ the Priest

Memorize the following catechism answer and Bible memory verse:

### Catechism Question

'How does Christ fulfil the office of a priest?'

### Answer

'Christ fulfils the office of a priest by offering himself once as a sacrifice to satisfy the Father's righteous anger against sin, thereby reconciling us to God, and interceding for us now.'

**Check it out for yourself**

1. Read Hebrews 4:14-16. Why does the writer of Hebrews think Jesus is such a good High Priest?

2. Read Hebrews 7:23-25. According to these verses, why is Jesus such a good High Priest?

3. Read Hebrews 7:26-28. According to these verses, why is Jesus such a good High Priest?

4. Read Hebrews 9:1-10. According to these verses, what was the main task of the high priest?

5. Read Hebrews 9:11-14. What was the difference between the Old Testament sacrifices and Christ's sacrifice?

6. Read Hebrews 10:11-14. What is the difference between Old Testament priests and Jesus?

7. Read Hebrews 10:19-23. What should our response be to Christ as our High Priest?

### Memory Verse

'Such a high priest meets our need — one who is holy, blameless, pure, set apart from sinners, exalted above the heavens' (Heb. 7:26).

### Action

**Solomon's temple**

This is a drawing of a cross-section of the temple during the time of Solomon. Here the priests worked, led the people of Israel in worship, and sacrificed goats and bulls as offerings to God. On the

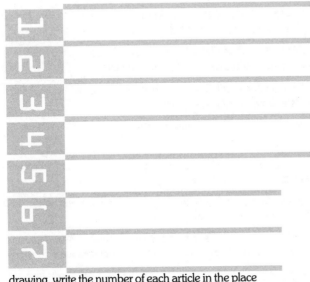

1
2
3
4
5
6
7

drawing, write the number of each article in the place
where it was found in the temple area.

1. Ceremonial washing
2. Table of consecrated bread
3. Ark of the covenant
4. The cherubim
5. Altar for sacrifices
6. Golden lampstands

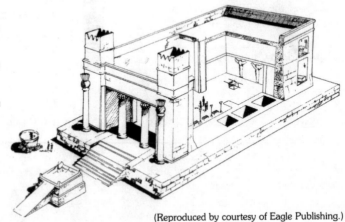

(Reproduced by courtesy of Eagle Publishing.)

## Christ the King

Memorize the following catechism answer and Bible memory verse:

### Catechism Question

'How does Christ fulfil the office of a king?'

### Answer

'Christ fulfils the office of a king by sub-duing us to himself, in ruling and defending us, and in restraining and conquering all his and our enemies.'

**Check it out for yourself**

1. Read Matthew 28:16-20. What kind of kingdom is King Jesus telling his subjects to establish in these verses?

2. Read 1 Corinthians 15:22-26. What will Jesus destroy before the end of human history? Who will be saved?

3. Read 2 Thessalonians 1:5-10. At his return what will King Jesus do to his enemies? And his friends?

4. Read Revelation 19:11-16. How do these verses describe King Jesus?

5. Read Revelation 20:11-15. According to these verses, what will King Jesus do in the future?

6. Read Revelation 21:1-8. According to these verses, what will King Jesus do in the future?

7. Read Matthew 19:27-30. At the end of time, when Jesus is seated on his royal throne, what can his followers look forward to?

### Memory Verse

'For he must reign until he has put all his enemies under his feet. The last enemy to be destroyed is death' (1 Cor. 15:25-26).

### Action

**Old Testament kings**

Israel remained a united nation for only a short time and had just three kings before being divided into two nations: Israel to the north and Judah to the south. Decide which nation each king ruled and then write the name of the king under the appropriate heading.

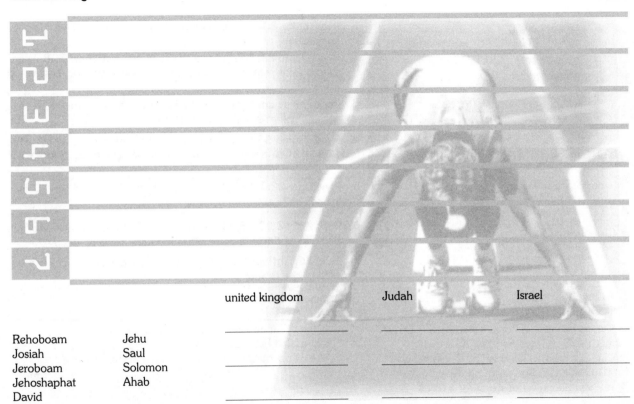

1
2
3
4
5
6
7

united kingdom       Judah       Israel

Rehoboam    Jehu
Josiah         Saul
Jeroboam     Solomon
Jehoshaphat   Ahab
David

## Christ's humiliation

Memorize the following catechism answer and Bible memory verse:

### Catechism Question

'What did Christ's humiliation consist of?'

### Answer

'Christ's humiliation consisted of his being born, and that under humble circumstances, under the Old Testament law; his experiencing the miseries of this life, the wrath of God, the curse of death on the cross, burial and the power of death for a time.'

**Check it out for yourself**

1. Read Luke 2:1-7. Explain how Christ's birth was part of his humiliation.

2. Read Galatians 4:4-5; Luke 2:27-28 and Matthew 5:18. What do you think it meant for Jesus to live under the Old Testament law?

3. Read Philippians 2:3-8. What was the attitude of Christ in these verses? What should your attitude be?

4. Read Isaiah 53:1-12. This Old Testament prophecy indicates several ways in which the Lord would be humiliated. State what they are.

5. Read Luke 22:39-46. According to these verses, why was Jesus in anguish?

6. Read Acts 2:22-28, 31-32. What did God the Father do for his Son? Was Christ's body subject to any form of decay?

7. Read 1 Corinthians 15:3-4. Which message is of primary importance in the Bible?

### Memory Verse

'And being found in appearance as a man,
    he humbled himself
        and became obedient to death — even death on a cross!'

(Phil. 2:8).

1 2 3 4 5 6 7

( Action )  **Scenes of humility**

On a posterboard or a large piece of paper, draw a picture depicting the biblical concept of humility. Your example could be of a missionary endeavour, an ordinary, modern-day example of humility, or a story from the Bible. Be prepared to share your ideas with others.

## Christ's exaltation

Memorize the following catechism answer and Bible memory verse:

### Catechism Question

'What does Christ's exaltation consist of?'

### Answer

'Christ's exaltation consists of his rising again from the dead on the third day, his ascension up into heaven, his sitting at the right hand of God the Father and his coming to judge the world at the last day.'

**Check it out for yourself**

1. Read Revelation 22:12-16. According to verse 14, how should one prepare for the coming of Jesus?

2. Read 1 Corinthians 15:20-26. How is Christ exalted (or glorified) in these verses?

3. Read Matthew 17:1-9. According to verse 9, what was the transfiguration pointing to?

4. Read Philippians 2:9-11. After Christ's humiliation (Phil. 2:6-8), what did God the Father do?

5. Read Revelation 1:4-8. When the exalted King comes again how will the world respond to his return?

6. Read Revelation 5:1-8. How does this passage describe the exalted Christ?

7. Read Revelation 5:9-14. What is the response of every creature in heaven to the exalted Christ?

### Memory Verse

'Therefore God exalted him to the highest place
and gave him the name that is above every name'

(Phil. 2:9).

1
2
3
4
5
6
7

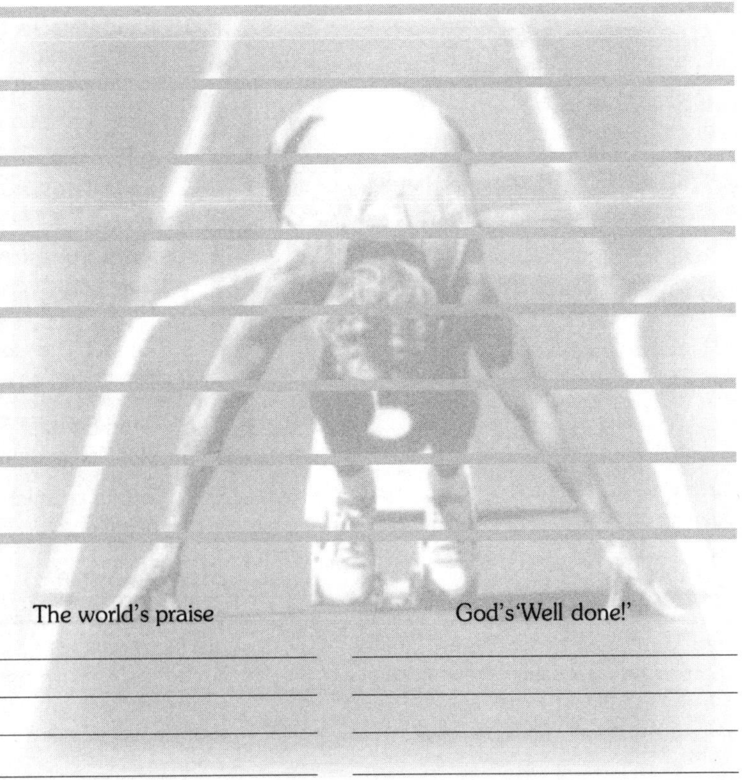

(Action) **Two perspectives on exaltation**

In the first column opposite list things someone may do in order to receive recognition from the world (in order to be praised or exalted). In the second column list things a Christian may do in order to receive God's 'Well done!'

The world's praise

God's 'Well done!'

## Redemption

Memorize the following catechism answer and Bible memory verse:

### Catechism Question

'How are we able to partake in the redemption purchased by Christ?'

### Answer

'We are able to partake in the redemption purchased by Christ, by the Holy Spirit who effectually applies it to us.'

**Check it out for yourself**

1.  Read Romans 8:9-11. According to these verses, what did the Spirit accomplish in the life of Christ? And what will he accomplish in you?

2.  Read Ephesians 1:11-14. List, in order of sequence, the steps which lead to a person's being saved.

3.  Read Titus 3:3-7. How does the Holy Spirit apply Christ's work to our lives?

4.  Read Ephesians 3:14-19. From these verses, what does the Spirit do for us? According to these verses, where does our faith come from?

5.  Read 2 Thessalonians 2:13-15. Which two things are necessary for Christ's redemption to be applied to a person's life?

6.  Read Ezekiel 36:24-28. In the Old Testament what was God's plan for redemption?

7.  Read Jeremiah 31:31-34. What difference will the new covenant bring?

### Memory Verse

'Repent and be baptized, every one of you, in the name of Jesus Christ for the forgiveness of your sins. And you will receive the gift of the Holy Spirit' (Acts 2:38).

### Action

**The Mandinka**

Nene cuddled her baby son. Outside her mud-and-thatch house the village people were singing and dancing. The marabout (Muslim teacher) had come, and Nene had paid him to tie ten jujus (charms) around Oumar's arms, neck and waist. She hoped these would keep him safe

1
2
3
4
5
6
7

from sickness and evil spirits, and bring him good luck. Nene sighed. The charms hadn't worked for her other three babies. They had all become sick and died. Nene had wanted to take the children to the Christian nurse at the nearby clinic, but her husband wouldn't let her. 'They will make you take off the jujus and burn them,' he told her, 'then the children will have no protection from the evil spirits.

We have to follow our Mandinka ways.' The marabout makes jujus from pieces of paper which have the name of a demon and a verse from the Koran written on them. The people believe these jujus are very powerful, and that the power comes from Allah, the Muslim God. Almost half the people living in the small West African country of the Gambia are Mandinkas. There are not

many Mandinka Christians yet. Missionaries try to show them that God loves them and can set them free from the power and fear of evil spirits. Some missionaries have translated the New Testament into Mandinka. They want the Mandinka to know that when they trust in Jesus, the Holy Spirit enters their lives and darkness flees (from *You Too Can Change the World*).

## Justification

Memorize the following catechism answer and Bible memory verse:

### Catechism Question

'What is justification?'

### Answer

'Justification is an act of God's free grace received by faith alone, by which he pardons all our sins and accepts us as righteous in his sight.'

**Check it out for yourself**

1. Read Romans 3:22-26. According to these verses, how can God justify his actions in saving sinners?

2. Read Romans 3:27-28 and 4:1-5. Can God save us because we try to keep his commandments or because we try to be good? Explain.

3. Read Romans 5:1-2 and 6-11. How does God justify not being angry with us even though we are sinners?

4. Read Romans 8:30-33. If you face accusations because you are a Christian, should that antagonism be expressed to you or to God? Why?

5. Read Luke 18:9-12. How would you describe the Pharisee in these verses?

6. Read Luke 18:13. How would you describe the tax collector?

7. Read Luke 18:14. Why was the tax collector justified? Why is Christ's death on the cross necessary for our justification?

### Memory Verse

'For all have sinned and fall short of the glory of God, and are justified freely by his grace through the redemption that came by Christ Jesus' (Rom. 3:23-24).

### Action

**Justification by grace through faith**

In John Bunyan's book *Pilgrim's Progress*, there is a man who has a great burden on his back. That man is named 'Christian'. Bunyan describes Christian as a burdened man, but then tells us that

1
2
3
4
5
6
7

'Christian ran to a place somewhat ascending and upon that place stood a cross, and a little below, in the bottom, a tomb. So I saw in my dream, that just as Christian came up to the cross, his burden loosed from off his shoulders, and from off his back, and began to tumble, and so continued to do so until it came to the mouth of the tomb where it fell in, and I saw it no more.'

sin, joy, assurance, fear, judgement, life,

righteousness, death, heaven, hell

Five of the words listed above are associated with 'Christian' before he was justified by grace through faith. Underline them. The other five refer to 'Christian' after he had become a follower of Christ. Circle them.

## Adoption

Memorize the following catechism answer and Bible memory verse:

### Catechism Question

'What is adoption?'

### Answer

'Adoption is an act of God's free grace, by which we are received into the family of God, and have a right to all the privileges which belong to the children of God.'

1. Read Romans 8:12-17. According to these verses, how can we know we have been adopted into the family of God?

2. Read Galatians 4:1-5. How do we become part of the family of God?

3. Read Galatians 4:6-7. How do we know we are true children of God? What is an heir (v. 7)?

4. Read John 8:31-41. Did the people listening to Jesus believe they were already part of the family of God? Why did they think that?

5. Read John 8:42-47. Did Jesus think his listeners were part of his family? Why?

6. Read 1 John 3:1-3. How can we get ready for meeting Jesus when he returns? Why?

7. Read 1 John 4:7-12. How should God's children act towards one another? How is this possible?

### Memory Verse

'How great is the love the Father has lavished on us, that we should be called children of God! And that is what we are!' (1 John 3:1).

### Action

**Adoption**

A husband and wife, Mr and Mrs Johnson, have been blessed by being able to adopt a little girl named Anna. The infant had been in an orphanage, but she is now part of the Johnson family. In the first column (opposite page)

1
2
3
4
5
6
7

list some of the benefits and privileges Anna now receives, which she would not previously have enjoyed. In the second column list some of the blessings which this new member of the family has brought to Mr and Mrs Johnson. Then discuss this by comparing the adoption of a child with the adoption of a person into the family of God. What are the similarities? What are the differences?

Anna's privileges

_____

_____

_____

_____

The Johnson's benefits

_____

_____

_____

_____

## Sanctification

Memorize the following catechism answer and Bible memory verse:

### Catechism Question

'What is sanctification?'

### Answer

'Sanctification is the work of God's free grace, by which he renews every part of us in his image, enabling us increasingly to die to sin and to live for righteousness.'

**Check it out for yourself**

1. Read Romans 8:1-11. According to verses 5-7, what is the main difference between Christians and non-Christians?

2. Read Romans 8:12-16. Are we able to put to death the misdeeds of the body in our own strength? Explain.

3. Read Ephesians 4:20-32. With the Spirit's power available to us, what are we commanded to do?

4. Read Romans 6:11-14. According to these verses, what is sanctification?

5. Read 2 Thessalonians 2:13-17. What are some of the ways in which we become sanctified?

6. Read 2 Peter 1:3-4. What has God given us that we may be sanctified?

7. Read 2 Peter 1:5-9. List the characteristics that we should add to the faith God has given us.

### Memory Verse

'For if you live according to the sinful nature, you will die; but if by the Spirit you put to death the misdeeds of the body, you will live' (Rom. 8:13).

### Action — A fruitful Christian life

Think of two trees, each bearing different fruit. Galatians 5:16-26 tells us that they are in conflict with each other. One tree produces fruit (actions) from the sinful nature. The other tree produces

1
2
3
4
5
6
7

fruit (actions) from a nature which is controlled by the Holy Spirit. Based on Galatians 5:19-23 write down six characteristics which each tree exhibits.

Holy Spirit

Sinful nature

## Death

Memorize the following catechism answer and Bible memory verse:

### Catechism Question

'What benefits do believers receive from Christ at death?'

### Answer

'At their death the souls of believers are made perfect in holiness and immediately pass into glory; and their bodies, being still united to Christ, rest in their graves until the resurrection.'

**Check it out for yourself**

1. Read 1 Corinthians 15:12-19. What is the guarantee that the bodies of Christians will be raised from the dead?

2. Read 1 Corinthians 15:20-26. The souls of believers immediately enter into the presence of God. When are their souls and bodies reunited?

3. Read 1 Corinthians 15:35-38. The apostle Paul tells us that when the Christian dies the body is like a seed of wheat. What does God do with our earthly bodies?

4. Read 1 Corinthians 15:39-44. How do the bodies we have now compare with the spiritual bodies God plans to give us at the resurrection?

5. Read 1 Corinthians 15:45-49. Who is the 'last Adam'? What are the differences between the two 'Adams'?

6. Read 1 Corinthians 15:50-55. What will happen to our bodies when Jesus comes again?

7. Read 1 Corinthians 15:56-58. As we are sinful, how can we receive resurrection bodies? How should we respond?

### Memory Verse

'We are confident, I say, and would prefer to be away from the body and at home with the Lord' (2 Cor. 5:8).

### Action

**A mystery**

According to the Bible, when Christians die they go to heaven to be with Jesus (2 Cor. 5:1-10). 1 Thessalonians 4:13-15 teaches us that when Jesus returns, these people will accompany him. But then in 1 Thessalonians 4:16, the Bible talks

1
2
3
4
5
6
7

about the dead in Christ rising from the grave. How is it that they return with Christ, and yet are raised by him from the dead? Use the space provided to explain this mystery!

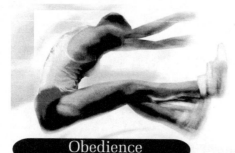

## Obedience

Memorize the following catechism answer and Bible memory verse:

### Catechism Question

'What is the duty which God requires of man?'

### Answer

'The duty which God requires of man is obedience to his revealed will.'

**Check it out for yourself**

1.  Read 1 Samuel 15:1-6. Would you describe this as war or judgement? What is the difference?

2.  Read 1 Samuel 15:7-11. What was wrong with Saul's actions?

3.  Read 1 Samuel 15:12-13. What was wrong with Saul's actions?

4.  Read 1 Samuel 15:14-21. Why was Saul's excuse unacceptable?

5.  Read 1 Samuel 15:22-23. According to Samuel, what is rebellion?

6.  Read 1 Samuel 15:24-26. What was the consequence of Saul's disobedience?

7.  Read 1 Samuel 15:27-29. According to these verses, what is God like?

### Memory Verse

'He has showed you, O man, what is good.
    And what does the LORD require of you?
To act justly and to love mercy
    and to walk humbly with your God'
                                    (Micah 6:8).

### Action                    Consequences

Obedience to God's revealed will always brings blessing and great joy. Disobedience always brings God's displeasure and results in a loss of joy. Listed opposite are Bible verses which mention people who either

| | Person | Action | Consequence |
|---|---|---|---|
| Acts 12:19-23 | | | |
| Genesis 22:9-18 | | | |
| 2 Samuel 6:1-7 | | | |
| Luke 1:5-7, 23-25 | | | |

obeyed or disobeyed, and which give the results of their actions. Look up the verses and write down whether the person (or people) obeyed or not. Briefly explain the consequence of their actions.

## Time to review

This is another important week — a week to review your work! I am sure that your teacher would like you not only to have perfect recall of all the catechism answers and Bible memory verses from this term, but also from last term! It gives the Saviour pleasure when you know the Word which he has given you. Find someone who is willing to test you on your memory work. Remember, by committing this work to memory, you are making an investment for eternity.

**Week 14**:   Q: 'What offices does Christ fulfil as our Redeemer?'

A: 'Christ, as our Redeemer, fulfils the offices of a prophet, a priest and a king, both while he was on earth and now in heaven.'

Verse:

'For to us a child is born,
to us a son is given,
and the government will be on his shoulders.
And he will be called
Wonderful Counsellor, Mighty God,
Everlasting Father, Prince of Peace'

(Isa. 9:6).

**Week 15**:   Q: 'How does Christ fulfil the office of a prophet?'

A: 'Christ fulfils the office of a prophet because he has revealed to us, by his Word and Spirit, the will of God for our salvation.'

Verse: 'No one has ever seen God, but God the one and only, who is at the Father's side, has made him known' (John 1:18).

**Week 16:**   Q: 'How does Christ fulfil the office of a priest?'

A: 'Christ fulfils the office of a priest by offering himself once as a sacrifice to satisfy the Father's righteous anger against sin, thereby reconciling us to God, and interceding for us now.'

Verse: 'Such a high priest meets our need — one who is holy, blameless, pure, set apart from sinners, exalted above the heavens' (Heb. 7:26).

**Week 17:**   Q: 'How does Christ fulfil the office of a king?'

A: 'Christ fulfils the office of a king by subduing us to himself, in ruling and defending us, and in restraining and conquering all his and our enemies.'

Verse: 'For he must reign until he has put all his enemies under his feet. The last enemy to be destroyed is death' (1 Cor. 15:25-26).

**Week 18:**   Q: 'What did Christ's humiliation consist of?'

A: 'Christ's humiliation consisted of his being born, and that under humble circumstances, under the Old Testament law; his experiencing the miseries of this life, the wrath of God, the curse of death on the cross, burial and the power of death for a time.'

Verse:

'And being found in appearance as a man,
he humbled himself
and became obedient to death — even death on a cross!'

(Phil. 2:8).

**Week 19:** Q: 'What does Christ's exaltation consist of?'

A: 'Christ's exaltation consists of his rising again from the dead on the third day, his ascension up into heaven, his sitting at the right hand of God the Father and his coming to judge the world at the last day.'

Verse:

'Therefore God exalted him to the highest place
and gave him the name that is above every name'

(Phil 2:9).

**Week 20:** Q: 'How are we able to partake in the redemption purchased by Christ?'

A: 'We are able to partake in the redemption purchased by Christ, by the Holy Spirit who effectually applies it to us.'

Verse: 'Repent and be baptized, every one of you, in the name of Jesus Christ for the forgiveness of your sins. And you will receive the gift of the Holy Spirit' (Acts 2:38).

**Week 21:** Q: 'What is justification?'

A: 'Justification is an act of God's free grace received by faith alone, by which he pardons all our sins and accepts us as righteous in his sight.'

Verse: 'For all have sinned and fall short of the glory of God, and are justified freely by his grace through the redemption that came by Jesus Christ' (Rom. 3:23-24).

**Week 22:** Q: 'What is adoption?'

A 'Adoption is an act of God's free grace, by which we are received into the family of God, and have a right to all the privileges which belong to the children of God.'

Verse: 'How great is the love the Father has lavished on us, that we should be called children of God! And that is what we are!' (1 John 3:1).

**Week 23:** Q: 'What is sanctification?'

A: 'Sanctification is the work of God's free grace, by which he renews every part of us in his image, enabling us increasingly to die to sin and to live for righteousness.'

Verse: 'For if you live according to the sinful nature, you will die; but if by the Spirit you put to death the misdeeds of the body, you will live' (Rom. 8:13).

**Week 24:** Q: 'What benefits do believers receive from Christ at death?'

A: 'At their death the souls of believers are made perfect in holiness and immediately pass into glory; and their bodies, being still united to Christ, rest in their graves until the resurrection.'

Verse: 'We are confident, I say, and would prefer to be away from the body and at home with the Lord' (2 Cor. 5:8).

**Week 25:** Q: 'What is the duty which God requires of man?'

A: 'The duty which God requires of man is obedience to his revealed will.'

Verse:

'He has showed you, O man, what is good.
    And what does the LORD require of you?
To act justly and to love mercy
    and to walk humbly with your God'

(Micah 6:8).

# Third Quarter

You are now half way through the course. I trust you learned the first twenty-six catechism answers and Bible memory verses really well! Keep revising them so that you don't forget them! The Ten Commandments are dealt with in the third quarter. Knowing the commandments, understanding their meaning and purpose, and assessing your life against the high standard of God's law will make you a strong and faithful Christian. Although believers do not have the strength themselves to keep these laws, the Holy Spirit helps them to obey God's moral law.

## The Ten Commandments

Memorize the following catechism answer and Bible memory verse:

### Catechism Question

'What is the sum of the Ten Commandments?'

### Answer

'The sum of the Ten Commandments is: To love the Lord our God with all our heart, with all our soul, with all our strength and with all our mind; and our neighbour as ourselves.'

**Check it out for yourself**

1. Read Mark 12:28-34. Why did the man speaking to Jesus mention burnt offerings and sacrifices?

2. Read Matthew 5:43-48. Why does Jesus tell us to love our enemies?

3. Read Luke 10:25-28. What is necessary in order to inherit eternal life?

4. Read Luke 10:29. Why did this man need to justify himself?

5. Read Luke 10:30-32. What was noteworthy about the fact that the priest and the Levite did not help the injured man?

6. Read Luke 10:33-35. What was noteworthy about the fact that the Samaritan helped the injured man?

7. Read Luke 10:36-37. What is Jesus teaching us here?

### Memory Verse

'Jesus replied: "'Love the Lord your God with all your heart and with all your soul and with all your mind.' This is the first and greatest commandment. And the second is like it: 'Love your neighbour as yourself.' All the Law and the Prophets hang on these two commandments'" (Matt. 22:37-40).

Action          **Dilemma**

Vilas was proud to be Serbian. He had always hated the Albanians because he believed that they had stolen his people's land. After Vilas became a believer in the Lord Jesus Christ, he learned from Scripture that he was to love his enemies. But the Scriptures also taught him that he should obey those in authority over him. Recently, his leaders called upon him to fight against the Albanians. If he refuses to fight, it is certain that he will face imprisonment. What do you think he should do?

## The only true God

Memorize the First Commandment and catechism answer:

### Catechism Question

'What is required in the First Commandment?'

### Answer

'The First Commandment requires us to know and acknowledge God to be the only true God, and our God, and to worship and glorify him accordingly.'

**Check it out for yourself**

1. Read Exodus 32:1-4. What is it about idolatry that angers God intensely?

2. Read Exodus 32:5-6. What happened after this act of pagan worship?

3. Read Exodus 32:7-10. What is the Lord planning to do in these verses? Why?

4. Read Exodus 32:11-14. According to Moses, to whom did the people belong? On what basis did Moses say this?

5. Read Exodus 32:15-25. What were the consequences of the people's disobedience?

6. Read Exodus 32:26-30. What was the consequence of their sin? Who makes atonement (v. 30) for sin?

7. Read Exodus 32:31-35. How does God show both judgement and mercy in these verses?

### Memory Verse

'You shall have no other gods before me' (Exod. 20:3).

### Action

The Lord declares in Matthew 6:31-33: 'So do not worry, saying, "What shall we eat?" or "What shall we drink?" or "What shall we wear?" For the pagans run after all these things, and your heavenly Father knows that you need them.

1
2
3
4
5
6
7

But seek first his kingdom and his righteousness, and all these things will be given to you as well.' Christ's warning is that things (food, clothing, sports, work, fashion, recreation, cars, etc.) can become 'gods' when they absorb more and more of our time and attention. God commands: 'You shall have no other gods before me.'

**Dilemma**

★ Manuel is an outstanding football player. He is also a Christian. He has just been nominated to play for the national team in the World Cup. As far as he knows there are no other Christians in the team. Practices will take place every day, and he will be away from his family and his church (where he is an elder) for nearly a year. Manuel loves football, but is concerned that it has become a temptation, a 'god', in his life. What do you think he should do?

## Idolatry forbidden

Memorize the Second Commandment and the catechism answer:

### Catechism Question

'What is required in the Second Commandment?'

### Answer

'The Second Commandment requires that we observe and keep pure all religious worship that God has commanded in his Word.'

**Check it out for yourself**

1. Read Isaiah 44:6-8. How do these verses describe the Lord?

2. Read Isaiah 44:9-20. How do the idols described in these verses compare with the Lord?

3. Read Isaiah 40:15-26. How do the idols described in these verses compare with the Lord?

4. Read Deuteronomy 4:1-8. According to verse 7, what is the difference between the true and living God and false gods?

5. Read Deuteronomy 4:9-14. When God gave the Ten Commandments the people saw no form; they only heard a voice. Why?

6. Read Deuteronomy 4:15-24. Are we permitted to make an image of God? Explain.

7. Read Deuteronomy 4:25-31. What can keep us from falling into idolatry?

### Memory Verse

'You shall not make for yourself an idol... You shall not bow down to them or worship them; for I, the Lord your God, am a jealous God...' (Exod. 20:4-6).

### Action

The catechism answer tells us that we should observe and keep pure all religious worship that God has commanded in his holy Word. The Scriptures make it clear that it is essential for us to be well taught so that our worship of the Lord will be pure and right. When we do

**1**
**2**
**3**
**4**
**5**
**6**
**7**

not know our Bibles or God's commandments, it is easy for us to fall into idolatry. Before he ascended into heaven, Jesus commanded his disciples to 'teach them to obey everything I have commanded you' (Matt. 28:20). Obedience to the Word of God will keep our worship pure, and will protect us from idolatry.

**Dilemma**

✳ Priya is the only Christian in her Hindu family. Each year her large family gathers to
✳ observe Diwali, the Hindu 'Festival of Lights', which celebrates the victory of light
✳ over darkness and of good spirits over evil spirits. The festival is a time of feasting and fireworks, music and dancing. Her family always forms a parade, and goes
✳ down to the river where her mother offers coconuts and bananas to a Hindu goddess whom the family believes will bring them good luck. Should Priya celebrate
✳ with her family, or should she refuse and risk being shunned by them?

**Reverence for God's name**

Memorize the Third Commandment and the catechism answer:

**Catechism Question**

'What is required in the Third Commandment?'

**Answer**

'The Third Commandment requires the holy and reverent use of God's names, titles, attributes, ordinances, word and works.'

**Check it out for yourself**

1. Read Deuteronomy 28:58-63. Write down two things which God is concerned about in these verses.

2. Read Psalm 68:4. Mention three ways in which God's name is properly revered.

3. Read Revelation 15:3-4. Write down several reasons for revering God's name.

4. Read Malachi 1:6-14. How is God's name being misused in these verses? How does God want his name to be used?

5. Read Psalm 138:1-3. Mention two things for which King David praises God.

6. Read Job 36:22-26. Which of God's attributes are we called upon to praise?

7. Read Revelation 5:11-14. How do the angels honour the name of God in heaven?

**Memory Verse**

'You shall not misuse the name of the LORD your God, for the LORD will not hold anyone guiltless who misuses his name' (Exod. 20:7).

**Action**                      **Dilemma 1**

When Pastor Chang mentioned from the pulpit that he was displeased with the language some of the people were using, he caught John's attention. The pastor said that slang words like 'geez' and 'God' were inappropriate words for Christians to use. John had never before

1
2
3
4
5
6
7

### Dilemma 2

considered himself to be misusing God's holy name when he used words like these. Do you think the pastor was being over-critical, or do you think he was right?

✿ Susan goes to church with her family most Sundays. She has attended many worship services where the Lord's Supper has been observed. She never hesitates to partake of the elements (the bread and the cup). She is confident that she knows and loves the Lord Jesus, but her mind always wanders during this part of the worship service. Do you think that she is misusing the Lord's name, or breaking the Third Commandment? How can Susan improve her worship during communion?

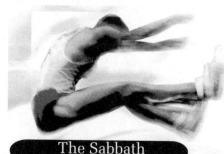

## The Sabbath

Memorize the Fourth Commandment and the catechism answer:

**Catechism Question**

'What is required in the Fourth Commandment?'

**Answer**

'The Fourth Commandment requires that we keep holy to God one whole day in seven, to be a holy Sabbath to himself.'

**Check it out for yourself**

1. Read Genesis 2:1-3. Why do you think God rested on the seventh day?

2. Read Exodus 16:19-31. Does God want us to keep the Fourth Commandment? With reference to this passage, explain your answer.

3. Read Isaiah 58:13-14. What motivation is there for keeping the Sabbath?

4. Read Nehemiah 13:15-22. Do you think Nehemiah was too hard on the merchants? What was his motive?

5. Read Luke 4:14-19. What did Jesus do on the Sabbath?

6. Read Matthew 12:1-14. What other activities was the Lord willing to do on the Sabbath?

7. Read Acts 20:7; Matthew 28:1-6; 1 Corinthians 16:1-2 and Revelation 1:10. Why do you think the Sabbath was changed from Saturday to Sunday?

**Memory Verse**

'Remember the Sabbath day by keeping it holy. Six days you shall labour and do all your work, but the seventh day is a Sabbath to the Lord your God...' (Exod. 20:8-11).

**Action**

Many Christians today give little, or no, consideration to the Fourth Commandment. For them, Sunday is no different from any other day of the week. However, God gave the Lord's Day for our benefit. We should refrain from engaging in our normal day-to-day activities in

1
2
3
4
5
6
7

order to remember the Lord especially on his day. We spend six days of the week working, playing, attending school, etc., but Sunday should be resolutely set aside for worship, prayer and praise. This still allows for other activities on the Lord's Day. We sin if we neglect to make the day holy, and if we choose worldly activities rather than spiritual ones.

## Dilemma

❖ Steve comes from a good Christian home. His family has devotions each morning. On Sundays they spend time after the evening service discussing both the morning
❖ and evening sermons. But now Steve has been offered a part-time, weekend job which is well paid. If he accepts it, he will have to leave church before the Sunday
❖ morning service is over, and will not be home until late on Sunday evening. Steve knows he will need the money when he goes to university next year. What do you
❖ think he should do?

## Honouring our parents

Memorize the Fifth Commandment and the catechism answer:

**Catechism Question**

'What is required in the Fifth Commandment?'

**Answer**

'The Fifth Commandment requires that we preserve the honour of others and fulfil our responsibility to them whether they are superior, inferior, or equal in their relationship to us.'

**Check it out for yourself**

1. Read Deuteronomy 21:18-21. Why did God impose such a harsh sentence on a rebellious son?

2. Read Matthew 15:3-9. In Christ's illustration, what had the man done to dishonour his parents?

3. Read Ephesians 6:1-4. Who are the superiors and inferiors in these verses and what is their responsibility to each other?

4. Read Ephesians 6:5-9. Who are the superiors and inferiors in these verses and what is their responsibility to each other?

5. Read Ephesians 5:21-32. Are there superiors and inferiors in this relationship? What is their responsibility to each other?

6. Read 1 Peter 2:13-17. Why is it important to submit to and show proper respect for the people mentioned in these verses?

7. Read Romans 12:9-16. What should our attitude be to others, especially those of humble status?

**Memory Verse**

'Honour your father and your mother, so that you may live long in the land the LORD your God is giving you' (Exod. 20:12).

**Action**                    **Dilemma**

Linda, age twenty-two, and Mike, age twenty-four, plan to get married next year. Both are committed Christians who have been praying about serving the Lord on the mission field by using their

1
2
3
4
5
6
7

medical training. But Linda's parents are strongly opposed to the marriage. They believe Mike is stealing their daughter and taking her far away from them. They are threatening not to attend the wedding or to pay any of the expenses associated with it. They refuse to let Mike come to their home, and openly speak against him. What are some of the issues which Linda and Mike face because of this dilemma? How does the Fifth Commandment apply to this situation? What do you think Mike and Linda should do?

## Do not murder

Memorize the Sixth Commandment and the catechism answer:

### Catechism Question

'What is required in the Sixth Commandment?'

### Answer

'The Sixth Commandment requires all lawful efforts to preserve our own life and the life of others.'

**Check it out for yourself**

1. Read Ephesians 5:28-30. How should we regard our bodies?

2. Read 1 Kings 18:2-4. In spite of great danger, what had Obadiah done?

3. Read Acts 16:25-34. How did Paul keep the Sixth Commandment?

4. Read Genesis 4:1-12. What do you think Cain's motive was for killing his brother Abel?

5. Read Genesis 9:5-6. Why is murder unacceptable to God?

6. Read Matthew 5:21-26. What does Jesus condemn in us? How does Jesus tell us to deal with conflict?

7. Read James 3:13 - 4:3. According to these verses, what is another cause of murder?

### Memory Verse

'You shall not murder' (Exod. 20:13).

### Action
**Thoughts to ponder**

Anger, malice, selfish ambition and envy are all characteristics which destroy us by making us bitter and resentful. They even cause us to think murderous thoughts. What do these situations show us about anger?

1
2
3
4
5
6
7

* A young man, aged nineteen, had a fight with his girlfriend. He drove away in his father's car at a very high speed, failed to negotiate a bend in the road and was killed.
* A parent regularly hit a child so hard that she was severely injured. Later the little girl died because of her injuries.
* A doctor has discovered that more than fifty diseases, including severe ulcers, are caused by anger.

Christ came into the world to free us from such sinful behaviour. The Spirit of God can produce in us good fruit which will last for eternity. What do these verses say about resisting a spirit of anger: Psalm 37:8; Proverbs 10:12; 10:18; 15:17; 15:18; 16:32; 17:1; 22:24-25; 25:28; Ecclesiastes 7:9; 1 Corinthians 13:4-7; Philippians 4:8; Colossians 3:8; James 1:19-20?

## Sexual purity

Memorize the Seventh Commandment and the catechism answer:

### Catechism Question

'What is required in the Seventh Commandment?'

### Answer

'The Seventh Commandment requires the preservation of our own and our neighbour's chastity, in heart, speech and behaviour.'

**Check it out for yourself**

1. Read 2 Samuel 11:1-5. What were the steps that led to David's adultery?

2. Read 2 Samuel 11:6-16, 25-27. How did David try to cover up his sin?

3. Read 2 Samuel 12:1-14. What was God's judgement on David for his sin?

4. Read Psalm 51:1-12. After the prophet Nathan exposed David's sin, how did David respond?

5. Read Genesis 39:1-23. How did Joseph respond to temptation?

6. Read Matthew 5:27-30. Does Jesus really want us to cut off our right hand? What is he saying here?

7. Read 1 Corinthians 6:12-20. Why must we flee sexual immorality?

### Memory Verse

'You shall not commit adultery' (Exod. 20:14).

### Action — A Christian understanding of sexual morality

'But among you there must not be even a hint of sexual immorality, or of any kind of impurity...' (Eph.    . he struggle ith sexual temptation is fierce. o maintain sexual purity is difficult, even for people  ho live in a setting  here the

biblical ideal is upheld and, to a high degree, maintained. But e live in a culture that tolerates (and even encourages young people being sexually active. We live in a society that uses sex to sell products on television, in books, films and music. All taboos have been removed. Even homosexual activity is increasingly vie ed as acceptable behaviour. No one seems to be listening to the Lord's voice as he speaks to us in the Bible.

A person trying to live a morally pure life before God is bombarded daily ith a different message. Many churches have given up trying to maintain biblical standards. Instead of offering forgiveness to repentant sinners, some churches appear to be telling people that sex outside of marriage is acceptable. Yet e are called to a higher and better life. God's la has not changed. He calls us to sexual purity. Sex should be confined to marriage.

King David paid a high price for his sexual immorality. Joseph as greatly rearded for remaining pure. Joseph as the one ith the clear conscience, ho enjoyed immense favour from God. Be a are of the messages you receive from films, music and on television. Cling to the standards laid do n in the Bible. You ill never regret it.

## Do not steal

Memorize the Eighth Commandment and the catechism answer:

### Catechism Question

'What is required in the Eighth Commandment?'

### Answer

'The Eighth Commandment requires that we obtain and increase our wealth and the wealth of others lawfully.'

**Check it out for yourself**

1. Read Joshua 7:1-12. After their victory at Jericho, the Israelites were defeated at a city called Ai. Why were they defeated?

2. Read Joshua 7:13-21. Why was God so angry about Achan's theft?

3. Read Joshua 7:22-26. Why did they spread the stolen goods out before the Lord?

4. Read Deuteronomy 22:1-4. What is one person's responsibility to the property of another person?

5. Read Proverbs 23:20-21 and 28:19-22. What should our attitude be to work and the pursuit of wealth?

6. Read Ephesians 4:28. What is the main reason we should work and not steal?

7. Read 1 Timothy 6:6-10, 17-19. In these verses we read that our goal should be Christian contentment. How do we achieve contentment? What temptations should we avoid?

### Memory Verse

'You shall not steal' (Exod. 20:15).

### Action

**Dilemma**

Jill received honours at university for coming first in her class of graduates. Her dark secret is that she cheated in several of her final exams. As a result of coming first, she won a scholarship and is now

1 2 3 4 5 6 7

studying for a higher degree at a prestigious university. She is doing well academically. She thinks that she would probably have had excellent results in her exams, even if she hadn't seen copies of the papers ahead of time. Through a student evangelistic group, she has come to trust Jesus Christ as Lord. Her Christian fellowship group has asked her to speak to them on the topic 'Christian integrity in the exam room'. What should Jill do? What might it cost her to tell the truth?

## Telling the truth

Memorize the Ninth Commandment and the catechism answer:

### Catechism Question

'What is required in the Ninth Commandment?'

### Answer

'The Ninth Commandment requires that we maintain and promote truth between persons, upholding our own and our neighbour's good name, especially in witness-bearing.'

## Check it out for yourself

1. Read John 10:22-39. What commandment did the Pharisees accuse Jesus of breaking? What is blasphemy?

2. Read John 8:12-18. Mention two persons who were willing to testify that Jesus is the light of the world.

3. Read John 8:42-47. Why were those listening to Jesus unable to understand what he was saying? What was their father like?

4. Read John 8:48-59. It was impossible for Jesus to lie. Was it costly for Jesus to tell the truth? Explain.

5. Read Acts 5:1-11. Who is the dark agent behind our lies? Why do you think the judgement of Ananias and Sapphira was so harsh?

6. Read 3 John 9-12. Compare Diotrephes and Demetrius in their keeping of the Ninth Commandment. What testimony did others have of them?

7. Read Psalm 15. Who can have access to God, and dwell with the Lord for ever?

### Memory Verse

'You shall not give false testimony against your neighbour' (Exod. 20:16).

### Action

There are times when telling the truth seems almost impossible because of the potential pain and cost. The people wanted to kill Jesus because he always told the truth. Jesus claimed to be God

1
2
3
4
5
6
7

### Dilemma

and so the religious leaders of his day accused him of blasphemy (John 10:33). They hated Jesus because he truthfully condemned them for their hypocrisy.

- Juan saw Mark wearing an expensive leather jacket. He was jealous, and started a rumour that Mark had stolen it. Maria knew that Mark had bought the jacket with money he had earned from a part-time job, but she was afraid to contradict Juan.
- How have Juan and Maria failed to obey the Ninth Commandment? How do jealousy and peer pressure keep you from obeying the Ninth Commandment?

## Do not covet

Memorize the Tenth Commandment and the catechism answer:

### Catechism Question

'What is required in the Tenth Commandment?'

### Answer

'The Tenth Commandment requires full contentment with our own condition, with a charitable frame of spirit towards our neighbour, and all that is his.'

**Check it out for yourself**

1.  Read 1 Kings 21:1-16. In which ways did the covetous hearts of Ahab and Jezebel show themselves?

2.  Read Acts 8:9-24. What did Simon the sorcerer covet? In which ways did his covetous heart show itself?

3.  Read Hebrews 13:5. If we love money, is it possible to be content? How does money rob us of contentment?

4.  Read Romans 7:7-10. The commandment says, 'Do not covet.' What does this tell us about ourselves?

5.  Read 1 Corinthians 13:4-7. What attitudes should we show towards our neighbours?

6.  Read Luke 12:13-21. What is Jesus teaching us in this parable?

7.  Read Romans 13:8-10. When do we know that we are successful in keeping the commandments?

### Memory Verse

'You shall not covet your neighbour's house. You shall not covet your neighbour's wife, or his manservant or maidservant, his ox or donkey, or anything that belongs to your neighbour' (Exod. 20:17).

### Action

**Dilemma**

Lance struggled with an inferiority complex. Although he had grown up in a Christian family, he had never found the Christian life very interesting. What concerned Lance more than anything was himself. He suffered from a poor self-image. He spent a lot of time alone

because he thought that nobody would want to be with him. He wanted to be more like his classmates who were out-going, but he was quiet and reserved. He wanted to excel at sports, but he doubted he would get into any of the teams. He wanted to be like a couple of the boys in his class who always kept others laughing, and never seemed to have difficulty conversing with the girls. He was envious of those who got high marks in school. Secretly, Lance was angry that everyone else seemed to excel at something. To put it biblically, Lance coveted what he did not have. If you could help Lance, what would you say to him? What positive things from this lesson would you share with him? What can Lance do to overcome his covetous attitude?

## Keeping the commandments

Memorize the following catechism answer and Bible memory verse:

### Catechism Question

'Is anyone able to keep the commandments of God perfectly?'

### Answer

'No one since the fall of Adam and Eve is able to keep the commandments of God perfectly, but daily breaks them in thought, word and deed.'

**Check it out for yourself**

1. Read Romans 3:9-18. How many people are righteous? In God's sight how bad are we?

2. Read Romans 3:19-20. What is the purpose of the law (the Ten Commandments)?

3. Read Romans 3:21-24. If the law condemns us, how are we set free from the law?

4. Read 1 John 1:8-10. What do you think it means to 'confess'?

5. Read Genesis 6:5-7. What is the Lord's opinion of our hearts? Do you think the Lord will judge the earth again?

6. Read Galatians 5:16-18. Why is it impossible for us to keep the law in our own strength?

7. Read Romans 6:11-14. How does grace free us from the law?

### Memory Verse

'If we claim to be without sin, we deceive ourselves and the truth is not in us' (1 John 1:8).

### Action

Unscramble each of the words to form a verse which is found in the book of Galatians. Then, in your own words, explain what you think the verse means.

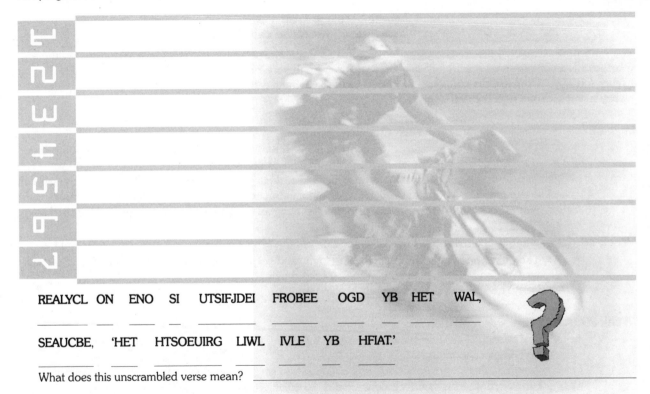

REALYCL ON ENO SI UTSIFJDEI FROBEE OGD YB HET WAL,

\_\_\_\_\_ \_\_ \_\_\_ \_\_ _____ _____ \_\_\_ \_\_ \_\_\_ \_\_\_\_,

SEAUCBE, 'HET HTSOEUIRG LIWL IVLE YB HFIAT.'

_____ \_\_\_ _____ \_\_\_\_ \_\_\_\_ \_\_ \_\_\_\_\_.'

What does this unscrambled verse mean? _____

## Time to review

You have now completed the study of the Ten Commandments. Knowing the commandments and hiding them in your heart is an investment for a lifetime. There is great reward in keeping them. Be sure that you don't forget the first twenty-four catechism answers and memory verses. Go over them and say them to your friends or family. Here's the review material. You know the drill!

**Week 27:**    Q: 'What is the sum of the Ten Commandments?'

A: 'The sum of the Ten Commandments is: To love the Lord our God with all our heart, with all our soul, with all our strength and with all our mind; and our neighbour as ourselves.'

Verse: 'Jesus replied: "'Love the Lord your God with all your heart and with all your soul and with all your mind.' This is the first and greatest commandment. And the second is like it: 'Love your neighbour as yourself.' All the Law and the Prophets hang on these two commandments"' (Matt. 22:37-40).

**Week 28:**    Q: 'What is required in the First Commandment?'

A: 'The First Commandment requires us to know and acknowledge God to be the only true God, and our God, and to worship and glorify him accordingly.'

Verse: 'You shall have no other gods before me' (Exod. 20:3).

**Week 29:**    Q: 'What is required in the Second Commandment?'

A: 'The Second Commandment requires that we observe and keep pure all religious worship that God has commanded in his Word.'

Verse: 'You shall not make for yourself an idol... You shall not bow down to them or worship them; for I, the Lord your God, am a jealous God...' (Exod. 20:4-6).

**Week 30:**  Q: 'What is required in the Third Commandment?'

A: 'The Third Commandment requires the holy and reverent use of God's names, titles, attributes, ordinances, word and works.'

Verse: 'You shall not misuse the name of the LORD your God, for the LORD will not hold anyone guiltless who misuses his name' (Exod. 20:7).

**Week 31:**  Q: 'What is required in the Fourth Commandment?'

A: 'The Fourth Commandment requires that we keep holy to God one whole day in seven, to be a holy Sabbath to himself.'

Verse: 'Remember the Sabbath day by keeping it holy. Six days you shall labour and do all your work, but the seventh day is a Sabbath to the Lord your God...' (Exod. 20:8-11).

**Week 32:**  Q: 'What is required in the Fifth Commandment?'

A: 'The Fifth Commandment requires that we preserve the honour of others and fulfil our responsibility to them, whether they are superior, inferior, or equal in their relationship to us.'

Verse: 'Honour your father and your mother, so that you may live long in the land the LORD your God is giving you' (Exod. 20:12).

**Week 33:**  Q: 'What is required in the Sixth Commandment?'

A: 'The Sixth Commandment requires all lawful efforts to preserve our own life and the life of others.'

Verse: 'You shall not murder' (Exod. 20:13).

**Week 34:** Q: 'What is required in the Seventh Commandment?'
A: 'The Seventh Commandment requires the preservation of our own and our neighbour's chastity, in heart, speech and behaviour.'
Verse: 'You shall not commit adultery' (Exod. 20:14).

**Week 35:** Q: 'What is required in the Eighth Commandment?'
A: 'The Eighth Commandment requires that we obtain and increase our wealth and the wealth of others lawfully.'
Verse: 'You shall not steal' (Exod. 20:15).

**Week 36:** Q: 'What is required in the Ninth Commandment?'
A: 'The Ninth Commandment requires that we maintain and promote truth between persons, upholding our own and our neighbour's good name, especially in witness-bearing.'
Verse: 'You shall not give false testimony against your neighbour' (Exod. 20:16).

**Week 37:** Q: 'What is required in the Tenth Commandment?'
A: 'The Tenth Commandment requires full contentment with our own condition, with a charitable frame of spirit towards our neighbour, and all that is his.'
Verse: 'You shall not covet your neighbour's house. You shall not covet your neighbour's wife, or his manservant or maidservant, his ox or donkey, or anything that belongs to your neighbour' (Exod. 20:17).

**Week 38:**  Q: 'Is anyone able to keep the commandments of God perfectly?'
A: 'No one since the fall of Adam and Eve is able to keep the commandments of God perfectly, but daily breaks them in thought, word and deed.'
Verse: 'If we claim to be without sin, we deceive ourselves and the truth is not in us' (1 John 1:8).

# Fourth Quarter

## The wrath of God

Memorize the following catechism answer and Bible memory verse:

### Catechism Question

'What does every sin deserve?'

### Answer

'Every sin deserves God's wrath and curse, both in this life, and that which is to come.'

Check it out for yourself

1. Read Romans 1:18-32. How does God's wrath reveal itself in people's lives? What are some of the ways God punishes people in this life for their sin?

2. Read Ephesians 5:3-7. According to these verses, what kind of behaviour brings God's wrath?

3. Read Ephesians 2:1-3. How does God regard us if we are not Christians?

4. Read Psalm 2:1-6. When the kings of the earth take their stand against King Jesus, how does Jesus respond to them?

5. Read Psalm 2:7-12. What should the kings of the earth do, if they are wise?

6. Read Matthew 25:31-40. At the end of time what will God's sheep receive? Why?

7. Read Matthew 25:41-46. At the end of time what will the goats receive? Why?

### Memory Verse

'No immoral, impure or greedy person — such a man is an idolater — has any inheritance in the kingdom of Christ and of God' (Eph. 5:5).

### Action

**Jonathan Edwards (1703-1758)**

Jonathan Edwards was the only son in a family of twelve children. He was born in East Windsor, Connecticut. After studying at Yale College he became a pastor, and was a person used greatly by God to bring about spiritual awakening in

## Sinners in the hands of an angry God

America. While much of his preaching centred on the love of God and our enjoyment of him, Edwards preached on every aspect of God's character and from every part of the Bible. Below is an excerpt from his most famous sermon, 'Sinners in the hands of an angry God', in which he preached on the fearful consequences of experiencing God's wrath and judgement:

'There is nothing that keeps wicked men at any one moment out of hell, but the mere pleasure of God... The use of this awful subject may be for awakening unconverted persons to a conviction of their danger... The bow of God's wrath is bent, and the arrow made ready on the string; and justice directs the bow to your heart... Therefore, let everyone that is out of Christ, now awake, and flee the wrath to come. The wrath of Almighty God is now undoubtedly hanging over every unregenerate sinner. Let everyone flee out of Sodom — escape for your lives, look not behind you, escape to the mountain lest you be consumed.'

## Faith

Memorize the following catechism answer and Bible memory verse:

### Catechism Question

'What is faith in Jesus Christ?'

### Answer

'Faith in Jesus Christ is a saving grace by which we receive and rest upon him alone for salvation, as he is offered to us in the gospel.'

**Check it out for yourself**

1. Read Ephesians 2:4-9. These verses describe God saving sinners by his grace. Where does faith come from?

2. Read Hebrews 10:35-39. How did these Christians prove that they had real faith?

3. Read Hebrews 11:8-19. Name three situations where Abraham demonstrated faith in God. How does each situation demonstrate his faith?

4. Read Hebrews 12:1-3. Why is Jesus 'the author and perfecter of our faith'?

5. Read Matthew 8:5-13. Why did Jesus think the centurion had such great faith?

6. Read Matthew 15:21-28. Why did Jesus think the Canaanite woman had such great faith?

7. Read Acts 16:12-15. Who preached the gospel of salvation to Lydia? Who gave Lydia faith to believe? How did Lydia demonstrate that she had faith in Christ?

### Memory Verse

'Yet to all who received him, to those who believed in his name, he gave the right to become children of God' (John 1:12).

### Action
**Faith**

On the opposite page there are three examples where faith is demonstrated. Next to each explain how faith is applied in the situation.

1
2
3
4
5
6
7

Every day Mrs Jones crosses a bridge in her car.

This woman is sitting on a bench.

This man has just become a Christian.

## Repentance

Memorize the following catechism answer and Bible memory verse:

### Catechism Question

'What is repentance?'

### Answer

'Repentance is a saving grace, by which a sinner, out of a true sense of his sin, and a realization of the mercy of God in Christ, with grief and hatred of his sin, turns from it to God, fully intending to endeavour to live a life of new obedience.'

## Check it out for yourself

1. Read Jeremiah 3:19-21. How did the LORD describe his relationship with his people Israel?

2. Read Jeremiah 3:22-25. How did the people respond to God's statement about their relationship?

3. Read 2 Corinthians 7:8-11. Which two kinds of sorrow and repentance does Paul mention?

4. Read Acts 2:36-41. How do we know that the people listening to Peter were repentant?

5. Read Matthew 3:1-6. How did the people demonstrate true repentance?

6. Read Matthew 3:7-12. What kept the Pharisees and Sadducees from repenting?

7. Read Psalm 51:10-17. David's repentance was sincere. How can you tell?

### Memory Verse

'Return, faithless people;
    I will cure you of backsliding.'

'Yes, we will come to you,
    for you are the LORD our God'
                              (Jer. 3:22).

### Action — The prodigal son and repentance

Listed opposite is a series of events which occurred in the religious experience of the prodigal son. From Luke 15:11-32, recreate the story in the correct order in which the events occurred in the young man's life. Write down the corresponding verse from Luke 15.

| 1 | |
| 2 | |
| 3 | |
| 4 | |
| 5 | |
| 6 | |
| 7 | |

| | | | | |
|---|---|---|---|---|
| Severe famine | 1. _____ | Luke 15: _____ |
| Still a long way off | 2. _____ | Luke 15: _____ |
| Feeding pigs | 3. _____ | Luke 15: _____ |
| Comes to his senses | 4. _____ | Luke 15: _____ |
| Father shows compassion | 5. _____ | Luke 15: _____ |
| Gets together all he has | 6. _____ | Luke 15: _____ |
| Confesses his sin | 7. _____ | Luke 15: _____ |
| Wild living | 8. _____ | Luke 15: _____ |

## Reading the Word

Memorize the following catechism answer and Bible memory verse:

### Catechism Question

'How is the Word to be read and heard, that it may become effective in salvation?'

### Answer

'In order that the Word may become effective in salvation we must attend to it with diligence, preparation and prayer; receive it with faith and love, hide it in our hearts and practise it in our lives.'

### Check it out for yourself

1. Read Luke 8:4-14. Explain how the first three groups of people failed to make salvation effective in their lives.

2. Read Luke 8:15. How did Christ say we should hear the Word of God?

3. Read 2 Timothy 3:14-17. What was Paul's counsel to Timothy?

4. Read 2 Timothy 4:1-5. How diligently do most people hear the Word preached? Explain.

5. Read James 1:22-25. What is James' counsel to us?

6. Read Hebrews 3:16 - 4:2. Why did the people who were led out of Egypt not enter God's rest?

7. Read 1 Peter 1:22 - 2:3. What will the Word of God do for us?

### Memory Verse

'I have hidden your Word in my heart that I might not sin against you'
(Ps. 119:11).

### Action        Word puzzle

Fill in the missing words in the five verses on the opposite page. Then use letters from the corresponding numbers to complete the answer phrase.

1. Psalm 94:14 'the Lord will not _____ his people'

$\overline{13}$ $\overline{10}$ $\overline{19}$ $\overline{2}$ $\overline{3}$ $\overline{17}$

2. Psalm 17:8 '_____ me in the shadow of your wings'

$\overline{9}$ $\overline{5}$ $\overline{14}$ $\overline{7}$

3. Hebrews 3:7 'if you hear his ____ '

$\overline{6}$ $\overline{12}$ $\overline{16}$ $\overline{3}$ $\overline{4}$

4. Matthew 6:25 'do not ____ about your life'

$\overline{15}$ $\overline{12}$ $\overline{1}$ $\overline{13}$ $\overline{21}$

5. 1 Peter 1:7 'greater _____ than gold'

$\overline{11}$ $\overline{20}$ $\overline{1}$ $\overline{8}$ $\overline{18}$

**Answer:** '1  2  3  4  5  6  7    8  9  10    11  12  13  14    15  16  17  18    19  20  21'

## Prayer

Memorize the following catechism answer and Bible memory verse:

### Catechism Question

'What is prayer?'

### Answer

'Prayer is an offering up of our desires to God for things agreeable to his will, in the name of Christ, with confession of our sins and thankful acknowledgement of his mercies.'

**Check it out for yourself**

1. Read 1 John 5:14-15. What is the main requirement before prayer will be heard?

2. Read 1 John 3:21-24. Mention some other conditions which need to be met before our prayers will be heard.

3. Read Philippians 4:4-7. According to these verses, how should believers pray?

4. Read Psalm 32:1-6. What aspect of prayer does the psalmist emphasize here? What was the psalmist's situation? What was the Lord's response?

5. Read Mark 12:38-40. What was wrong with the prayers of the teachers of the law?

6. Read Acts 12:1-18. What are some of the truths about prayer which we can learn from this story?

7. Read Revelation 5:8 and 8:1-5. How important are our prayers to God?

### Memory Verse

'This is the confidence we have in approaching God: that if we ask anything according to his will, he hears us' (1 John 5:14).

### Action

An excellent way to form a prayer is to use the acronym 'ACTS'.

**Adoration**   Begin your prayer by worshipping God, adoring him for who he is. Think of God's many characteristics: his love, justice, wrath against sin, saving grace, holiness, etc. Meditate on the Lord's greatness; praise him and bring glory to his name.

**Confession**   Confess all known sins and seek pardon for them, as well as for unknown sins. Ask the Lord to cleanse you, making your prayers acceptable to him.

**Thanksgiving**   Give thanks for everything that the Lord has done for you.

**Supplication**   Make your requests known to God — not only personal requests, but also pray for the needs of others. Ask God to do things, both great and small, but always according to his will.

## Our Father in heaven

Memorize the following catechism answer and Bible memory verse:

### Catechism Question

'What does the preface to the Lord's Prayer teach us?'

### Answer

'The preface to the Lord's Prayer (which is "Our Father in heaven") teaches us to draw near to God with holy reverence and confidence, as children to a father who is able and ready to help us; and that we should pray with and for others.'

## Check it out for yourself

1. Read Matthew 6:5-8. Why does the Lord command us to pray in secret?

2. Read Romans 8:15-16. To whom are we to pray? What kind of relationship is it?

3. Read Mark 14:32-36. To whom did Jesus pray? What kind of relationship was it?

4. Read Luke 11:1-8. What is Jesus teaching us in verses 5-8? Why?

5. Read Luke 11:9-13. What is Jesus teaching us about his Father?

6. Read John 17:1-5. What is the burden of Jesus' prayer in these verses?

7. Read John 17:20-26. Whom is Jesus praying for?

### Memory Verse

'But when you pray, go into your room, close the door and pray to your Father, who is unseen. Then your Father, who sees what is done in secret, will reward you' (Matt. 6:6).

### Action
#### Postures in prayer

The verses listed on the opposite page mention different postures which can be adopted while at prayer. Write down your reaction to each of these. Do you adopt any of these postures when you pray?

1
2
3
4
5
6
7

Luke 22:39-46; Acts 21:3-6

Luke 18:13-14; Mark 11:22-25

1 Kings 18:36-40; Deuteronomy 9:15-21

## God's holy name

Memorize the following catechism answer and Bible memory verse:

### Catechism Question

'What do we pray for in the first petition?'

### Answer

'In the first petition (which is "Hallowed be your name") we pray that God would enable us and others to glorify him for who he is, and that he would work all things for his own glory.'

**Check it out for yourself**

1. Read 1 Peter 2:9-12. How are Christians described? What is their purpose?

2. Read Psalm 33. Mention several reasons given in this psalm why we should trust 'in his holy name' (v.21).

3. Read Psalm 96. What does hallowing God's name have to do with taking the gospel to the nations?

4. Read Acts 12:19-25. Why was Herod killed?

5. Read Matthew 2:1-12. How did the Magi glorify God's name?

6. Read Isaiah 6:1-5. What did Isaiah see? Why was he so dismayed?

7. Read Revelation 15:1-4. What will God's people do in heaven?

### Memory Verse

'Let them know that you, whose name is the LORD —
that you alone are the Most High over all the earth'

(Ps. 83:18).

### Action

**Cryptoquote**

Each of the letters in the phrase opposite represents a different letter of the alphabet. There is no particular pattern, but each letter represents another. To get you started we will give you two letters.

1
2
3
4
5
6
7

Wherever you see an 'S' in the puzzle substitute an 'L'. Wherever you see a 'Y' substitute an 'H'. Your final phrase will be a line from a well-known psalm.

F  S<small>FWA</small>,  FBW  S<small>FWA</small>,

\_\_  \_\_\_\_  \_\_  \_\_\_\_

YFH   ETRKLGQP   QL   NFBW   DTEK   QD   TSS   GYK   KTWGY!

\_\_\_  _____  \_\_  \_\_\_\_  \_\_\_\_  \_\_  \_\_\_  \_\_\_  \_\_\_\_\_!

## The coming kingdom

Memorize the following catechism answer and Bible memory verse:

### Catechism Question

'What do we pray for in the second petition?'

### Answer

'In the second petition (which is "Your kingdom come") we pray that Satan's kingdom may be destroyed; and that the kingdom of Christ may be advanced, ourselves and others brought into it and kept in it; and that Christ may return soon.'

**Check it out for yourself**

1. Read Luke 10:17-20. How was Satan's kingdom being defeated?

2. Read Ephesians 6:10-18. What weapons do we need to fight against the kingdom of Satan?

3. Read Matthew 13:24-30. What is Jesus teaching in this parable?

4. Read Matthew 13:44-46. What is Jesus teaching in these two parables?

5. Read Matthew 13:47-50. What is Jesus teaching in this parable?

6. Read Revelation 11:15-18. What is taking place in these verses?

7. Read Revelation 22:20. What should we pray for? Why?

### Memory Verse

'Behold, I am coming soon! My reward is with me, and I will give to everyone according to what he has done' (Rev. 22:12).

1
2
3
4
5
6
7

**Action**

Use the clues in the column on the right to complete the column in the middle.

1. _ _ _ **K**
2. _ **I** _ _ _
3. _ _ _ _ **N**
4. _ _ _ **G** _ _ _ _
5. _ _ _ **D** _ _ _
6. _ _ **O** _ _ _
7. _ _ _ **M** _ _ _ _

Clues:
1. Luke 12:31 '____ his kingdom'
2. Colossians 1:12 'the kingdom of ____ '
3. Revelation 11:15 '... and he will ____ for ever and ever'
4. Psalm 145:11 'the ____ of your kingdom'
5. 2 Thessalonians 1:5 'God's ____ is right...'
6. Matthew 16:28 'see the Son of Man ____ in his kingdom'
7. James 2:5 'the kingdom he ____ those who love him'

## The will of God

Memorize the following catechism answer and Bible memory verse:

### Catechism Question

'What do we pray for in the third petition?'

### Answer

'In the third petition (which is "Your will be done on earth as it is in heaven") we pray that God, by his grace, would make us able and willing to know, obey and submit to his will in all things, as the angels do in heaven.'

## Check it out for yourself

1. Read Psalm 103:19-22. What do the angels do in heaven?

2. Read Psalm 67. What is the psalmist hoping the nations will do?

3. Read Job 1:1-8. In God's sight, what kind of man was Job?

4. Read Job 1:9-19. Why did God allow Satan to test Job?

5. Read Job 1:20-22. What was Job's response to disaster?

6. Read Matthew 26:36-46. What was the essence of Christ's prayer when he was faced with death?

7. Read John 6:35-40. What was the Father's will for Jesus?

### Memory Verse

'I desire to do your will, O my God; your law is within my heart'
(Ps. 40:8).

### Action

The answers to these clues overlap. See how quickly you can fill them in! (Write your answers on the line, above the numbers.)

1 2 3 4 5 6 7

1-7     Revelation 4:11 'by your will they were _____ and have their being'
7-11    2 Timothy 2:26 '... escape from the trap of the _____'
11-13   Psalm 40:8 'Your ___ is within my heart'
13-17   Philippians 2:13 'for it is God who _____ in you'
17-26   1 Thessalonians 4:3 'it is God's will that you should be _____'
26-31   Psalm 40:8 'I _____ to do your will'
31-35   Hebrews 13:21 'May the God of peace _____ you with everything good for doing his will'
35-38   1 Thessalonians 5:16 '____ continually . . . for this is God's will for you'

1 2 3 4 5 6 7 8 9 10 11 12 13 14 15 16 17 18 19 20 21 22 23 24 25 26 27 28 29 30 31 32 33 34 35 36 37 38

## Daily provision

Memorize the following catechism answer and Bible memory verse:

### Catechism Question

'What do we pray for in the fourth petition?'

### Answer

'In the fourth petition (which is "Give us today our daily bread") we pray that by God's kindness we may receive a portion of the good things of this life, and enjoy his blessing with them.'

**Check it out for yourself**

1. Read Proverbs 30:7-9. Why should we request neither poverty nor riches?

2. Read Exodus 16:13-23. How much manna did the Lord provide for the people? Why?

3. Read John 6:43-51. What are the similarities between the manna in the desert and the Saviour?

4. Read John 6:52-58. What are the differences between the manna and the Saviour?

5. Read John 6:1-15. What does this story teach us about Christ?

6. Read 1 Timothy 6:6-10. What did Paul warn Timothy about?

7. Read Matthew 6:25-34. What does Jesus teach us about our desire for food and clothing?

### Memory Verse

'Keep falsehood and lies far from me; give me neither poverty nor riches, but give me only my daily bread'
(Prov. 30:7-8).

### Action

**George Müller**

George Müller was born in Prussia (now part of Germany) in 1805. After living a sinful life as a young person, he was wonderfully converted by God. Soon after his conversion he began his life's work of ministering to orphans. He

determined that all the children's needs would be met by faith and through prayer; no appeal for money would be made to anyone but God. His congregation agreed. At times they were down to their last coin, or even out of funds, before God answered prayer. The most well-known example of this occurred one morning at the breakfast table. With no food in the cupboard and no money left, Müller said grace: 'Dear Father, we thank thee for what thou art going to give us to eat'. As he finished praying the baker arrived with a supply of fresh bread; the Lord had told him during the night that it was needed. Then the milkman came; his cart had broken down and he asked them to take the milk so that he could do some repairs! By now Müller had 130 children to care for each day, and even though they had a simple lifestyle, it was secure; they never went without. 'Give us today...'

## Confession

Memorize the following catechism answer and Bible memory verse:

### Catechism Question

'What do we pray for in the fifth petition?'

### Answer

'In the fifth petition (which is "Forgive us our debts, as we also have forgiven our debtors") we pray that God would freely pardon all our sins, which we are encouraged to ask because by his grace we are enabled from the heart to forgive others.'

### Check it out for yourself

1. Read Psalm 51:1-4. What are some of the requests David made after he had sinned?

2. Read Psalm 51:5-12. What did David long for, which his sin had destroyed?

3. Read Psalm 51:13-17. What did David promise God he would do if he was forgiven?

4. Read Matthew 5:21-26. How important is it to seek forgiveness? Explain.

5. Read Matthew 18:21-22. What did Jesus mean when he said we should forgive seventy-seven times?

6. Read Matthew 18:23-35. What is the main teaching of this parable?

7. Read 1 John 1:8-9. What is the encouragement we receive from these verses?

### Memory Verse

'Have mercy on me, O God,
    according to your unfailing love;
according to your great compassion
    blot out my transgressions'
                        (Ps. 51:1).

### Action

**A chorus about confession**

Confession is good for the soul. It humbles us and makes us acknowledge our need of a Saviour. In the end, David could thank the Lord for

humbling him by causing him to acknowledge and confess his sinful behaviour (Ps. 32). When David kept silent God's hand was heavy upon him. Only confession brought blessed relief. Jesus tells us in the Beatitudes (Matt. 5:3-5) that people who mourn over their sin are blessedbecause they understand the need to confess their sin regularly to God.

Do you know the following chorus? It is David's confession taken from Psalm 51:10-12.

'Create in me a clean heart, O God,
and renew a right spirit within me.
Cast me not away from your presence, O Lord,
Take not your Holy Spirit from me;
Restore unto me the joy of your salvation,
And renew a right spirit within me.'

## Deliverance

Memorize the following catechism answer and Bible memory verse:

### Catechism Question

'What do we pray for in the sixth petition?'

### Answer

'In the sixth petition (which is "And lead us not into temptation, but deliver us from the evil one") we pray that God would either keep us from being tempted to sin, or support and deliver us when we are tempted.'

**Check it out for yourself**

1. Read James 1:13-14. Who is responsible for yielding to temptation? Why?

2. Read Genesis 22:1-18. Who was responsible for testing Abraham? Why?

3. Read Psalm 26. Should we ask God to test us? Why?

4. Read Genesis 39:1-10. How was Joseph able to resist sexual temptation?

5. Read Genesis 39:11-23. Did Joseph pay a price for his godly actions? How was Joseph blessed for remaining pure?

6. Read Matthew 4:1-11. How was Jesus able to resist temptation?

7. Read Psalm 119:9-16. How can we keep our way pure?

### Memory Verse

'Watch and pray so that you will not fall into temptation. The spirit is willing, but the body is weak' (Matt. 26:41).

### Action — Crossword puzzle

Complete the crossword, then unscramble the shaded letters to form a word central to this week's theme. Write the word on the line below.

_____

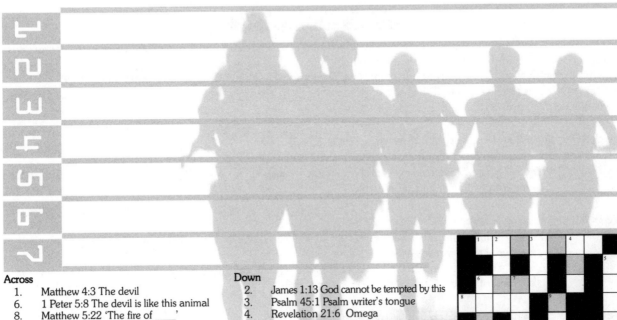

## Across
1. Matthew 4:3 The devil
6. 1 Peter 5:8 The devil is like this animal
8. Matthew 5:22 'The fire of ____'
10. Matthew 26:41 A way to avoid temptation
12. John 13:2 What the devil made Judas do
13. Matthew 6:22 The lamp of the body

## Down
2. James 1:13 God cannot be tempted by this
3. Psalm 45:1 Psalm writer's tongue
4. Revelation 21:6 Omega
5. Romans 16:20 What God will do to Satan
6. Hebrews 13:5 God will never do this
7. Luke 2:36 Anna's age
9. Matthew 26:41 How to avoid temptation
10. John 14:6 Jesus is the ____
11. Psalm 34:15 What God hears

## Time to review

Here it is — the final review session. To have memorized all forty-eight catechism answers and Bible memory verses is a great accomplishment. If you have applied yourself to your studies, there is no doubt that you will be well grounded in the basic doctrines of the Christian faith. Congratulations and well done! Don't put this book on the shelf to gather dust. From time to time, go over all that you have memorized so that you don't forget what you have learned. May God's blessing be upon you!

**Week 40:**  Q : 'What does every sin deserve?'

A : 'Every sin deserves God's wrath and curse, both in this life, and that which is to come.'

Verse : 'No immoral, impure or greedy person — such a man is an idolater — has any inheritance in the kingdom of Christ and God' (Eph. 5:5).

**Week 41:**  Q : 'What is faith in Jesus Christ?'

A : 'Faith in Jesus Christ is a saving grace by which we receive and rest upon him alone for salvation, as he is offered to us in the gospel.'

Verse : 'Yet to all who received him, to those who believed in his name, he gave the right to become children of God' (John 1:12).

**Week 42:**  Q : 'What is repentance?'

A : 'Repentance is a saving grace, by which a sinner, out of a true sense of his sin, and a realization of the mercy of God in Christ, with grief and hatred of his sin, turns from it to God, fully intending to endeavour to live a life of new obedience.'

Verse:
> 'Return, faithless people;
>> I will cure you of backsliding.'

> 'Yes, we will come to you,
>> for you are the LORD our God'

(Jer. 3:22).

**Week 43:**   Q: 'How is the Word to be read and heard, that it may become effective in salvation?'
A: 'In order that the Word may become effective in salvation we must attend to it with diligence, preparation and prayer; receive it with faith and love, hide it in our hearts and practise it in our lives.'
Verse:
> 'I have hidden your Word in my heart
>> that I might not sin against you'

(Ps. 119:11).

**Week 44:**   Q: 'What is prayer?'
A: 'Prayer is an offering up of our desires to God for things agreeable to his will, in the name of Christ, with confession of our sins and thankful acknowledgement of his mercies.'
Verse: 'This is the confidence we have in approaching God: that if we ask anything according to his will, he hears us' (1 John 5:14).

**Week 45:**   Q: 'What does the preface to the Lord's Prayer teach us?'
A: 'The preface to the Lord's Prayer (which is "Our Father in heaven") teaches us to draw near to God

with holy reverence and confidence, as children to a father who is able and ready to help us; and that we should pray with and for others.'

Verse : 'But when you pray, go into your room, close the door and pray to your Father, who is unseen. Then your Father, who sees what is done in secret, will reward you' (Matt. 6:6).

**Week 46:**   Q : 'What do we pray for in the first petition?'

A : 'In the first petition (which is "Hallowed be your name") we pray that God would enable us and others to glorify him for who he is, and that he would work all things for his own glory.'

Verse :

'Let them know that you, whose name is the LORD —
that you alone are the Most High over all the earth'

(Ps. 83:18).

**Week 47:**   Q : 'What do we pray for in the second petition?'

A : 'In the second petition (which is "Your kingdom come") we pray that Satan's kingdom may be destroyed; and that the kingdom of Christ may be advanced, ourselves and others brought into it and kept in it; and that Christ may return soon.'

Verse : 'Behold, I am coming soon! My reward is with me, and I will give to everyone according to what he has done' (Rev. 22:12).

**Week 48:**   Q : 'What do we pray for in the third petition?'

A : 'In the third petition (which is "Your will be done on earth as it is in heaven") we pray that God, by his grace, would make us able and willing to know, obey and submit to his will in all things, as the angels do in heaven.'

Verse:

> 'I desire to do your will, O my God;
>     your law is within my heart'

(Ps. 40:8).

**Week 49:**   Q: 'What do we pray for in the fourth petition?'

A: 'In the fourth petition (which is "Give us today our daily bread") we pray that by God's kindness we may receive a portion of the good things of this life, and enjoy his blessing with them.'

Verse:

> 'Keep falsehood and lies far from me;
>     give me neither poverty nor riches,
>     but give me only my daily bread'

(Prov. 30:7-8).

**Week 50:**   Q: 'What do we pray for in the fifth petition?'

A: 'In the fifth petition (which is "Forgive us our debts, as we also have forgiven our debtors") we pray that God would freely pardon all our sins, which we are encouraged to ask because by his grace we are enabled from the heart to forgive others.'

Verse:

'Have mercy on me, O God,
according to your unfailing love;
according to your great compassion
blot out my transgressions'

(Ps. 51:1).

**Week 51:**   Q: 'What do we pray for in the sixth petition?'

A: 'In the sixth petition (which is "And lead us not into temptation, but deliver us from the evil one") we pray that God would either keep us from being tempted to sin, or support and deliver us when we are tempted.'

Verse: 'Watch and pray so that you will not fall into temptation. The spirit is willing, but the body is weak' (Matt. 26:41).